PARTNERING INTELLIGENCE

PARTNERING INTELLIGENCE

*Creating Value for Your Business
by Building Strong Alliances*

Stephen M. Dent

·D|B· DAVIES-BLACK PUBLISHING
Palo Alto, California

PUBLISHED BY DAVIES-BLACK PUBLISHING
AN IMPRINT OF CONSULTING PSYCHOLOGISTS PRESS, INC.
3803 EAST BAYSHORE ROAD, PALO ALTO, CA 94303
800-624-1765

Special discounts on bulk quantities of Davies-Black books are available to corporations, professional associations, and other organizations. For details, contact the Director of Book Sales at Davies-Black Publishing, an imprint of Consulting Psychologists Press, Inc., 3803 East Bayshore Road, Palo Alto, CA 94303; 650-691-9123; Fax 650-623-9271.

03 02 01 00 99   10 9 8 7 6 5 4 3 2 1
Printed in the United States of America

Library of Congress Cataloging-in-Publication Data

Dent, Stephen M.
    Partnering intelligence : creating value for your business by building strong alliances / Stephen M. Dent. — 1st ed.
        p.   cm.
    Includes index.
    ISBN 0-89106-132-0 (hardcover)
    1. Strategic alliances (Business) I. Title.
HD69.S8D46   1999
658'.044—dc21   99–22739
                                                               CIP

FIRST EDITION
First printing 1999

*Dedicated to Hugh G. and Marie W. Dent
for teaching me the essence of partnering intelligence
and to Neal R. Holtan for his patience and love
while writing this book*

CONTENTS

CHARTS, EXERCISES, FIGURES, AND SURVEYS

FIGURES

SURVEYS

Of all of the dozens of business strategies available today, none offers both the potentially rich rewards and the devastating risks of partnership. While partnerships seem to offer the simplest and most direct path to success, failed partnerships litter the business landscape with broken dreams, financial loss, lost potential, and shattered relationships. Think about your most recent partnership. Perhaps it was with another organization, another department, or a colleague down the hall. How did it go? Was it good or bad for you? Why did it feel like that? Did you accomplish what you set out to do? What sorts of relationships did you form? What happened to make the partnership succeed or fail?

The ability to form partnerships is an important, even critical, skill in today's business environment. Yet for most of us, our partnerships evolve over time at an unconscious level. Why do we leave such an important aspect of our lives to happenstance? The desire to form partnerships is so ingrained in our psyche that most of us simply don't give it a second thought—we just do it. Yet despite our best intentions, most of us have experienced a failed partnership. We've been left alone wondering, What happened? What went wrong?

The answer lies in what I call *partnering intelligence.* Most of us understand the concept of IQ—our intelligence quotient. It's our innate ability to comprehend language, symbols, and logic as measured by a standardized test. It's one measure of how successful we will be in complex learning. In his recent best-seller, Daniel Goleman discusses the concept of emotional intelligence (EQ)—that is, our ability to delay immediate gratification and use self-control to attain a greater future outcome. Goleman points out fascinating discoveries in brain research proving that emotional stability may be more important than IQ in predicting a successful life. Each of us also has a partnering quotient (PQ)—or partnering intelligence. My experience with PQ demonstrates that people with certain attributes are more successful at navigating the complexities of creating successful and healthy partnerships. Using these attributes in conjunction with a special process for creating healthy partnerships increases their potential for success. This process is called the Partnership Continuum™. The Partnership Continuum is a blueprint that outlines the stages of task and relationship development that occur normally and naturally in all partnerships. This model can help you increase your partnering intelligence while exponentially improving your chances of creating a successful and mutually beneficial partnership for you and your business.

There are many books around that will tell you why partnering is an important business strategy. But *Partnering Intelligence* goes further by helping you determine your own partnering capabilities— and then giving you a blueprint to use in your organization. Along the way, you will learn about the six critical attributes of successful partnering and the tools you'll need to assess and improve your abilities in each of these attributes. You will learn, too, how you yourself can shape the success or failure of the partnering process within your business or organization.

What are your partnerships like today? Have you ever been in a situation where you didn't trust your partner? Have you ever felt your partner wasn't telling all? Have you resolved a conflict and then felt bad about how it ended? Did you ever want give someone some feedback but couldn't? If the answer to any of these questions is yes, then you'll want to read further. In the following chapters I address all these issues and more. And by the time we're finished, you'll have learned how to increase your PQ.

Stephen M. Dent

ACKNOWLEDGMENTS

This book would not have been possible without the help of literally hundreds of people. I apologize if I have missed anyone. You will know who you are. I want to thank all the people who helped me write this book including Susan Perry, Jeff Ostberg, Miles Canning, and Pamela Espeland for their guidance in the book's development; Laurie Harper, my agent, who had the insight to recognize the potential of this material and connect it and me with the right publisher; Jerry Martin for the years of work we did together to develop the Partnership Continuum model; Richard O. Johnson, Christine Matuzek-Rivas, Mary L. Taylor, and Susan Pisha for their support and belief in partnering. Thanks to Judy Olafsen for making me look better than I thought possible. Thanks also to my hundreds of clients and friends who every day teach me about partnering. A partial list includes John Dasburg, Pamela Hughes, Peter Mannetti, Richard McCormmick, Randy McPherson, Mary Lund, Bill Lewis, Jack Stack, Ed Stewart, Larry A. Wallace, Jack Welch, Kevin Wild, and Gary Wilson. Finally, thanks to Melinda Adams Merino, Laura Simonds, Jill Anderson-Wilson, and the folks at Davies-Black Publishing for their hard work and dedication to this project.

Legal Disclaimer

There are many types of partnerships. This book provides the reader with insights into the human attributes and dynamics that make individuals successful partners and the Partnership Continuum model, which helps groups of people create successful partnerships. This book does not address the legal aspects of partnerships. If you need help developing the legal aspects of a partnership, contact an attorney who specializes in legal partnerships in the state in which you live.

PART ONE

Rediscovering Partnering

Transitioning from "Me" to "We"

For as long as humans have populated this planet, we have struggled to survive. Along the way we learned that prosperity lay in banding together, determining what was in our best mutual interest, and moving forward in partnership. This strategy worked for thousands of years until the industrial age, when something fundamental changed in our society. As the industrial workplace became fragmented, functionalized, and specialized, we began to transition from banding together to looking out for ourselves individually. We forgot the importance of relationships that valued the "we" over the "me" as our work drove us farther and farther apart.

Now businesses all over the world are relearning this ancient partnering strategy. As our society and the global economy move from the postindustrial age into the age of information and communication, business leaders are awakening to the fact that they need to partner to survive. Because no one source contains all the information needed to operate in today's supercharged business climate, partnerships have become critical to the success of leaders and their businesses. But because this "partnering intelligence" that was kept alive for generations has been lost, they will need to rediscover and develop their partnering skills.

Part One describes the concept of partnering intelligence—what it is, why it's important, and how it affects your ability to build successful partnerships. Chapter One provides an overview of the Partnership Continuum model. It walks you through the four components of the model and explains why creating a smart partnership is a system and not an isolated event. It offers examples of how others have created smart partnerships for their businesses that their competitors cannot duplicate, thus providing them with a competitive edge. It explores the different types of partnerships and explains what works and what doesn't.

Chapter Two moves from the model to the individual, offering a self-assessment that will help you determine your partnering intelligence. Knowing where you stand is the first step toward increasing your partnering quotient, or PQ.

Partnering intelligence is not an innate intelligence, it's learned. Each of us has the capability to be a smart partner and build smart alliances. Part One will help you get a jump start on your competition and start adding value to your business by increasing your partnering intelligence.

CHAPTER ONE

Partnering Intelligence

What It Is and Why It's Important

Have you ever thought about the concept of *partnering intelligence?* Most of us don't spend a whole lot of time analyzing our partnerships, business or otherwise. They just happen. They evolve, and before we know it, they fall into a familiar pattern. They become part of our life's experience, both good and bad.

WHAT IS PARTNERING INTELLIGENCE?

Human beings are miraculously complex creatures. Each of us has a different way of viewing the world—a personal way of taking in information, processing it, and making decisions. We use a variety of skills and types of intelligence to help us through the complexities of life. These different types of intelligence confer different advantages to help us succeed. For example, your IQ (intelligence quotient) score on an intelligence test is a measure of your reasoning power, cognitive skills, and ability to verbalize and calculate. The IQ score, a measure of mental intelligence, is expressed as a number (quotient) on a scale from low to high. People with high IQ scores generally do well on tasks that require cognitive abilities. But a high IQ score is not the only measure of success.

Other kinds of intelligence influence our behavior and contribute to our success in achieving what we want and need in life. Emotional

3

intelligence (EQ), a term coined by Peter Salovey from Yale University and John Mayer from the University of New Hampshire in the early 1990s, is a measure of how well people solve problems and cope with challenges and adversity. Daniel Goleman, an expert in the field of emotional intelligence, writes about an experiment in which six-year-old children were offered two choices. Each child could choose to have one cookie right now, or two cookies later and no cookie now. Many years later, Goleman correlated other data from these same subjects with their choices in this experiment. His results indicate that the ones who chose to wait for the two cookies—those who were able to defer gratification—were generally more successful in their personal relationships and in their occupations.

The idea that different kinds of intelligence influence our decisions is obvious. A person's judgment and maturity are often more important than the factors measured with an IQ test. People with very high IQ scores but low EQ may have trouble coping with adversity, problem solving, and relationships despite all their mental aptitudes. Social scientists are discovering many other types of intelligence that serve us in different ways. While most of us excel in one or more areas, we may be lacking in other types of intelligence. In addition to mental, cognitive, and emotional intelligence, there is linguistic, logical, spatial, kinesthetic, and musical intelligence. The more we can master these various types of intelligence, the better equipped we will be to succeed in life.

Being successful in partnerships is a matter of applying a different kind of intelligence. Our partnering quotient (PQ) is a measure of our partnering intelligence—how well we can build relationships and cultivate trust while accomplishing predetermined tasks in an alliance with someone else. Partnering intelligence is our ability to succeed in partnership situations. We measure it by how well we are able to create and sustain healthy and mutually beneficial partnerships. We all have this ability. And we can all learn how to increase it.

How do you increase your partnering intelligence? You start by understanding yourself and evaluating your partnering skills. Partnering intelligence begins with self-awareness. This is the foundation for a strong partnership. Grounded in being well centered yourself and knowing your own needs, your partnering intelligence increases when you can identify and satisfy your partner's needs. When you personally guarantee you will do everything in your power to help your partner succeed, you are committed not only to your own success but to the success of the partnership, too. Your enterprise becomes an intelligent partnership when you are united in your dedication to each other's success while maintaining separate identities.

Once you have evaluated your own partnering skills, you need a process that will show you how to develop your partnering intelligence. I call this process the Partnership Continuum™: a deliberate, well-thought-out, scientific approach to creating partnerships. This model is used with others, within the context of a business or organization, to help individuals or groups of people move from "no partnership" to "full partnership." Using a step-by-step approach, the Partnership Continuum presents a framework so that partners can review and plan for the two major components—task and relationship—needed for successful partnerships. It defines the kind of atmosphere partnerships thrive in and utilizes the Plan–Do–Check–Act cycle for continuous improvement.

While most people and organizations will readily say they have formed relationships, for most of us the development of a truly cooperative partnership, based on mutual trust and benefit, remains an elusive goal. At times, even our personal relationships seem difficult at best. Fully developed partnerships are especially challenging in the business environment.

WHO NEEDS PARTNERSHIPS?

If partnership is so much work, why not simply go it alone? Census data reflecting current social trends show that many of us are single and are remaining single. Being single can mean being alone and being lonely. Loneliness is what moves people to endure the difficulties of the "dating game" in order to gain the love, companionship, and benefits that human relationships offer. In today's society, people who feel lonely and alienated from others can turn to a range of sources for relief: from therapists to advice columnists, from personal ads to clubs of all varieties, along with the myriad other distractions technology affords us. What people are craving is meaningful relationships.

The same is true for many businesses. They find themselves in need of other businesses—to expand their resources, to help with financing, to penetrate a new market, to develop or comarket a new product, or to defend their industry. They will go through the pain and risks of "dating" a few prospective partners. And indeed they may find a good fit for what they want—if they know how to go about it. Regardless of the situation, business or personal, in essence this is just normal human behavior. We feel a need and then we use the strategy of collaborating with someone else to help us fulfill it. Virtually all partnerships, personal and business, start out this way.

"Business happens only when people interact." Lots of companies and their employees misunderstand this business dynamic. At its most basic level, business is a transaction. The buyer needs a seller, a seller needs a buyer; at every level, in every instance, people transact. But too narrow a focus on one part of the business—such as the transaction—leads to imbalances that in turn lead to losses. This is because business is more than a transaction. Business happens not when the transaction occurs, but when people *interact*. One transaction could never sustain a business for very long. Successful, growing businesses are those that can create partnerships. By this I mean that they have the skill (the intelligence) to complete a task (a transaction) while developing a trustworthy and mutually beneficial relationship.

There are those who will tell you that new technologies drive business success. I disagree. Although technology can increase the speed or accuracy of a transaction, your competitors can rapidly replicate your new proprietary technology. Businesses can buy the technology they need, and the cost is less and the availability greater than ever before. All the conventional measures of business health look only at past results. The *future* prosperity of a business depends on its ability to initiate, sustain, and profit from interdependent relationships. Successful businesses develop relationships. Relationships can become creative partnerships and reflect the values of people working with trust and respect for each other. The outcomes of healthy partnerships among people are innovative products, creative services, and even new technology.

Most of us want to be part of something beyond ourselves. We yearn to have an ally we can rely on. Socially we need someone who supports us and in turn someone who needs and values our support.

For most of us, this is also true in business. We long to participate in a meaningful workplace where we are appreciated for our contributions. The "family spirit" of some companies is a powerful incentive for people to contribute. When market conditions change, businesses that have strong and trusting relationships among all the people who work for the company tend to cope better. Their sense of community helps them marshal resources and focus energy on mutual survival.

In 1996, a fire destroyed a textile mill in Massachusetts. The owner, after making sure the fire was out, went to his employees and comforted them. He told them they would rebuild the factory, promised them they would have jobs when the new factory was built, and made a truly extraordinary commitment. He told his employees they would continue to get paid until the new mill was finished. How do you think these employees felt about their boss and their company? One effect of their appreciation and loyalty was that they rebuilt the factory in record time—pitching in and doing jobs they had never done before, such as cleaning, helping with design, construction, and refurbishing the plant. By pulling together, the company even strengthened its sales relationships with customers and suppliers.

The kinds of partnerships businesses are looking for are the kinds that generate new energy. This energy is generated by a confluence of ideas, knowledge, and intelligences. We see examples of this dynamic every day. Our world is in constant flux, combining and recombining forces. New technologies evolve. When the nineteenth-century invention of the automobile joins with twentieth-century computer technology, the result is better running, more efficient, cleaner, cheaper automobiles.

Successful businesses create new products, services, strategies, and processes that satisfy or create new market needs. Innovative companies are constantly updating, expanding, and researching ways to perform in order to stay ahead of their competition and keep their customers satisfied. This process is becoming more and more challenging to handle alone. Advanced communication technologies have afforded us unprecedented access to information. In fact, we receive so much information that we have to rely on other people to help us keep up.

The contemporary pace of change reminds me of the famous *I Love Lucy* sketch in which Lucy and Ethel take jobs in a candy factory. As the conveyor belt speeds up, the increased workload overwhelms the two and candy ends up everywhere. This is how change is happening in business today. New responses to our changing perceptions replace the paradigms on which we've always relied. We replace our new paradigms when a new set of realities dictates it's time to change.

Because information is available in virtually every corner of the globe today through computer and telecommunication technologies, the world is now our marketplace, our research and development resource, our labor pool, and our source for capital. Companies everywhere are teaming up and multiplying their capacity to do business. Without partnerships, how can we possibly compete tomorrow?

Expanding Resources

A company that specializes in mass mailings may be able to complete a semiannual direct-mail marketing project for a small business more cheaply than the small business can accomplish the task itself. Does it make sense for the small company to hire mail room personnel, purchase and maintain database information systems, and add the expensive infrastructure needed for such a task if it sends out only two mailings a year? A software programming problem can be identified on Monday morning by a business in North America, it can be sent to India that evening, and a solution can be ready and waiting in North America on Tuesday morning. As the world grows smaller, the need for partners is more critical than ever before.

In many cases, we can't justify the cost of acquiring, developing, and maintaining the resources required to do it all. Businesses are reaching out to find partners with the expertise they need to provide the products and services their customers want. Consumer research shows that customers will switch to products or services that meet their personal needs, even if they have to pay more. As these needs become more sophisticated, businesses need the flexibility to customize their products and services. They need to be responsive to the customer, to be market driven, to retain their present customers and attract new ones. Many businesses turn to partnering as an essential strategy to help them accomplish their goals. Creating a successful partnership can be hard work, but the payoff can be huge and returns can come in unexpected ways. We form partnerships to access information or technology possessed by others. Partnerships can reenergize a business by bringing in new ideas and new methods for achieving results. Improved product quality, more efficient production, new avenues for marketing and sales—all may result from strategic partnerships.

Partnerships encourage creative innovations for improved product design and quality. When two separate groups merge, they bring with them different perspectives on how to accomplish something. Successful partnerships work with this diversity to produce a hybrid that is, in essence, the best of both. The key to reaping these benefits is creating an environment that stimulates creativity and risk taking—in which people feel safe trying out new concepts without fear of reprimand or punishment. The outcome is an innovation that neither group could have produced separately. It is a product of the vitality, creativity, diversity, and synergy partnerships are capable of generating.

One partnership that used synergy to beat the competition in the marketplace was a PCS wireless telephone company that partnered with a Baby Bell that provided landline service. The partners decided to combine the best of both services and offer customers features that no one else provided. How did they do this? The landline company knew its customers wanted only one telephone number to keep track of. The wireless company knew its customers wanted to take the phone with them wherever they went. So the companies offered the "wireless extension"—an innovation that acted like a home or office phone and that customers could answer in either location. In addition, their telephone handset mimicked a standard telephone that provided an immediate dial tone when activated. This partnership is wiping out the competition in the markets it serves.

Satisfying Customers

When organizations that have formed partnerships uniquely meet customer needs, they see their market share increase and their customer satisfaction ratings rise. When Northwest Airlines formed a partnership with KLM Royal Dutch Airlines, international travelers on both sides of the Atlantic were offered increased numbers of destinations. Beyond this added value, these international travelers benefited from such improvements as shared frequent flyer awards, improved reliability performance, and coordinated scheduling. Passengers saved time making connecting flights and were able to spend more time at either end of the trip—a considerable marketing advantage to Northwest–KLM's time-conscious business travelers.

As a direct result of their partnership, Northwest Airlines increased its pretax profits by $50 million a year and KLM enjoyed a healthy $150 million a year pretax profit increase. In December 1997, Northwest Airlines repaid a $39 million loan to the Metropolitan Airports Commission (MAC) in Minnesota more than fifteen years ahead of schedule. The loan was part of a $45 million package Northwest negotiated in 1992 with the State of Minnesota to save it from bankruptcy.

Reducing Expenses

Partnerships create unique opportunities to explore new and potentially valuable ways of reducing expenses. According to John Dasburg, president of Northwest Airlines, joint marketing programs generated most of the success in Northwest's partnership with KLM. A less heralded example of cooperation came from joint purchasing activities. Since early 1994, Northwest and KLM have engaged in sixty-nine successful joint procurement projects producing total savings of $31 million.

These projects, all nonstrategic in scope, reduced Northwest's expenses by $4.6 million in 1995, and future annual savings are estimated at $15 to $20 million. Furthermore, both airlines continue to expand cost-saving activities including sharing warehouse space at Schipol Airport in Amsterdam and joint ticketing and check-in counters at various other airports.

Increasing Productivity and Job Security

Tapping into everyone's creative knowledge results in a more viable and competitive organization. Meeting customer demands means more profitability, which translates into company growth and employee job security. When partnerships include unions or other employee groups, job productivity improves because of meaningful involvement in quality improvement. Inclusion enables a diverse workforce to contribute creative ideas and stimulates innovative ways of accomplishing tasks.

Saturn, the newest car division of General Motors, used this principle when starting up its manufacturing facility in Spring Hill, Tennessee. Partnering with the United Auto Workers (UAW), Saturn redesigned the manufacturing process of the Saturn automobiles. Today Saturn is ranked number one in quality for American cars by American consumers. Three components contributed to the Saturn partnership's success: innovative processes produced better cars; Saturn gained market share and customer loyalty; and the Saturn plant needed more employees. This meant more members for the UAW and more profits for General Motors.

Improving Relationships

Partnership helps organizations build better relationships—which benefits the organization internally and externally. As a consultant I've seen even the most broken processes meet customer requirements when internal relationships are good. But when processes are broken and the relationships are poor, woe to the customer, who is bound to suffer as a result of this combination.

Customer loyalty results from creating relationships with the customer. By establishing partnerships internally, organizations increase their skill at developing good relationships. Successful businesses do not create loyal customers only through price or quality advantages. These features can be quickly replicated by competitors. Customers want *relationships*. Customers who have a relationship with a business will be forgiving of mistakes where those without a relationship will walk. It costs about thirteen times more money to attract a new customer than to retain an old one. A loyal customer base, therefore, is much more profitable than even a huge potential market.

What engenders customer loyalty is the same partnering skills that employees practice with each other. Ritz-Carlton Hotels train their employees to behave as "ladies and gentlemen serving ladies and gentlemen." As we treat the people we work with, so we treat our customers. The same communication dynamics—including clear, respectful messages between managers and employees—will enhance customer satisfaction. The absence of good relationship skills in a company precludes the possibility of building good customer relations.

Organizations, businesses, nonprofits, communities, and even governments are coming to understand that in today's global world, "going it alone" is tough. Going it alone means an organization needs to provide everything for itself—which is impossible. Even the loner, the solo flier, and the maverick have at least superficial relationships. Businesses just can't exist without some kind of relationship with others. But just as the stereotypical one-night-stand character has fleeting relationships, so some businesses accumulate relationships that are shallow, temporary, and meaningless.

No matter how beneficial a partnership may be from a financial or transactional perspective, if the relationship isn't satisfying for the partners, the partnership will ultimately fail. Consider the analogy to personal relationships. Think of the number of people who have lowered their economic standard of living to get out of a bad marriage. People will leave the house, the money, the dog, and sometimes even the kids behind to escape the pain of a dysfunctional relationship. Sometimes even the threat of losing everything is not strong enough to convince partners to endure a marriage on the rocks. Divorce is the less painful alternative. Fortunately, another choice is available.

We can choose to change ourselves. We can commit to changing our attitudes and behavior. We can examine ourselves and work to revitalize the partnership. Easing the pain is one motivation for changing ourselves. Preserving what we've built together is an incentive for working hard on relationship issues. Just as a good counselor can help a dysfunctional marriage get back on track, a good business consultant can help fix a business partnership. But first the partners have to acknowledge the importance of the relationship. Then they can discover how to improve it.

TWO TYPES OF PARTNERSHIPS: EXTERNAL AND INTERNAL

A statement by Gary Wilson, chairman of Northwest Airlines, to the Press Club in Washington, D.C., describes a shift in thought about what constitutes a partnership. He said: "Mergers are out and alliances are in." He was referring to the proliferation of alliances recently announced by airline companies. In the first quarter of 1998

Northwest Airlines (already allied with KLM) declared alliances with Continental Airlines, Air Italia, Air France, and Cathay Pacific. In the same period, Delta allied itself with AeroPeru, and Nippon Airways formed alliances with United Airlines and Lufthansa. Wilson observed: "The airline industry is on a path to the future different from that followed by other industries. It is a path wary of mergers and acquisitions that make glittering projections about synergies and efficiencies. All too often these projections prove overly optimistic and difficult to achieve."

The type of partnership Gary Wilson was describing is what I call *external* partnership. I have worked with all sorts of external partnerships, from auto manufacturers and their suppliers to telephone companies and their unions. I have been involved in multipartner ventures on large construction jobs—partnerships involving building contractors, architects, trade unions, and building owners. All these efforts have one thing in common. They are all trying to achieve a task while developing a healthy and mutually beneficial partnership.

External partnerships can be extraordinarily rewarding. The Northwest–KLM partnership brought over $50 million worth of additional business to KLM at Schipol Airport alone in 1997. When the largest mall in the United States was built in suburban Minneapolis, thanks to partnerships it was finished three months ahead of schedule and $25 million under budget. In Minnesota a telephone company and its union were at odds over how to settle the scheduling of vacations. The two organizations sat down together and formed a partnership to figure out how to get the work orders completed during a busy summer season and still allow employees time off to enjoy the warm weather. Their partnership headed off a rash of "sick days" for the company and a huge backlog of grievances for the union. These are examples of the power of forming mutually beneficial partnerships.

I also help organizations develop *internal* partnerships. Internal partnerships are within a company. To me, the most basic business partnership is the partnership between the company and the people who work there. Certainly there is terrific potential in this relationship, but few companies recognize it as a partnership. Most take it for granted. Some companies think the employees just work there. But people want meaning and self-fulfillment from their work. They want cordial and respectful relations with the people they meet at work. They want to be part of the enterprise, part of a team, a value to the company. Companies and their employees can have a genuine, active, profitable partnership where everyone gets what they need—but only if they understand the principles of the partnering process and know how to increase their collective partnering intelligence.

Another area of huge potential is partnering between employees and departments within the company. In North America—and indeed in much of the industrialized world—business has been managed through compartmentalizing work by function. While this approach may have created some efficiencies when organizations were self-sufficient, the information age has made this practice obsolete. Businesses are recognizing that it is through cross-functional processes that customers get satisfied. If one function fails to live up to the customer's expectations, the whole organization looks bad. Ultimately, the entire organization pays the price for less than ideal customer service.

For an example, consider a client of mine: a wireless telephone company. Within the business, two departments—Sales Development and Order Fulfillment—were competing with each other to handle a piece of the process. Sales Development was responsible for ordering customer equipment based on customer requirements, industry trends, and the capabilities of manufacturing vendors. Order Fulfillment managed equipment inventory and shipped customer equipment from a warehouse once an order was received. The crux of the conflict was this: Who reordered equipment when inventory was low? While this may seem a simple inventory management issue, it was much more complex because of the product's nature. PCS or digital telephone handsets are a rapidly evolving product that is updated three or four times a year. Although the handset design itself may change only once or twice during a year, the software that runs the features is updated many times during the same period. Consequently, a new handset today can be rendered obsolete tomorrow by updated software. Order Fulfillment wanted to control inventory reordering. Since they were responsible for inventory cost and managing stock levels, this seemed to make sense. But since Sales Development had the relationship with the vendor, had access to industry trends, consumer tastes, and changes in network features, and understood the impact these factors had on the marketplace, Sales Development wanted to control the ordering process. The situation got so bad that it created animosity between the leaders in the organization. The essence of the situation boiled down to power and control. The power came from the inventory budget: money equals power and control. This is a fairly common dynamic in many organizations, one that can drive some pretty bizarre behavior.

When we brought the two groups together, they agreed to form a partnership. First we clarified the goals of these two organizations. And since the two goals were closely related—to make a profit and to satisfy the customer—we were able to align them quickly. Once we had a common goal we were able to redesign the equipment-ordering process so that each group was able to get its needs met. After working through their conflict, the team actually streamlined the process while reducing inventory overhead. This occurred over a period of about a month. In the end, the leaders of the two departments created a full partnership between the two divisions.

When companies respond constructively to employees' needs, they discover the keys to unleashing extraordinary energy, creativity, productivity, and loyalty. When companies partner with employees, productivity soars. Making the case for investing time, energy, and money in human resource development, however, is as tough a chore as ever because of the ways we've thought about business for the last two hundred years. But as we continue to evolve from the industrial age into the information age, our paradigm of human resources will need to change. This new age requires us to think about the intellectual capital humans create and how to cultivate it if we want to succeed in the future. The exponential growth in the sophistication of the technologies we use persuades us that this era is different from and presumably better than the industrial age. Yet many of our attitudes about how work should be done to maximize productivity haven't changed from the days when production workers monotonously repeated the same steps on the assembly line for thirty years.

On the brink of the millennium, many people are finding themselves alienated from each other and lacking in serious relationships— especially in the workplace. They are gravitating to companies where they can meet these needs. Businesses with an orientation to the past are finding themselves increasingly alone, struggling to find loyal employees, and fighting for their economic existence in the face of seemingly huge competitors. Other businesses with partnerships all over town, all over the country, and all over the world threaten the company that can't sustain relationships. The good news is that globally companies are changing, workforces are changing, and successful businesses are the ones that have figured out what partnering is all about. These are the companies people want to work for.

WHAT DOESN'T WORK

Some "partnerships" are not true partnerships but are more like forced marriages. Many organizations and businesses find themselves in situations that require them to deal with each other even though their relationships may be more adversarial than mutually beneficial. I recently had an opportunity to work with a huge quasigovernmental agency. As one of the largest employers in the world, it had many different unions and professional organizations representing its employees. One area vice president was trying hard to improve the workplace environment. To accomplish this monumental task, he wanted to form a partnership with the unions. Management understood that the best way to get to the root causes of employee unrest in the workplace was to get the employee unions to help them make improvements. But one of the most powerful unions—the one representing the bulk of this agency's employees—was so mistrustful of management that it refused to participate. During an exploratory meeting, the union came right out and said it did not believe management would address the problems fairly. Moreover, the union felt there was uneven power between management and employees. Then the union walked out of the discussion.

This was both unfortunate and fortunate. It was unfortunate that the union refused to work with management to improve the work environment for its membership. But it was fortunate for management's oversight committee since it clearly understood the union's position regarding their relationship. Since the union was not interested in being a partner, the committee could proceed without fear of being sabotaged

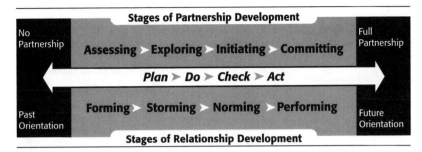

Figure 1 The Partnership Continuum Model

by a forced partner. The committee decided to leave the door open: If the union wanted to participate in the future, it could.

Forced marriages, although they sometimes appear successful, seldom work. Forced partners can harbor long-term animosity and resentment. I know of one company that merged more than a decade ago in which the employees still refer to each other by their previous company logos: "red tails" and "ducks." Generally speaking, partnerships are most successful when partners enter the relationship of their own free will.

THE PARTNERSHIP CONTINUUM MODEL

Knowing your partnering quotient and the attributes necessary for managing the partnership is only half of what you need for increasing your partnering intelligence. The other half is understanding the process of creating healthy, trusting, and mutually beneficial partnerships. Partnerships don't just happen. They are designed. The Partnership Continuum model (Figure 1) is the blueprint for creating successful partnerships. This model has been used successfully by thousands of people. It offers you and your partner a tested step-by-step approach in developing your partnership. By following the model you will increase your partnering intelligence by helping you and your partner to:

- Discuss the process to use in forming the partnership—thus opening communications and starting to build trust between you
- Begin creating a mutual vision

- Complete an internal needs assessment
- Start identifying each other's needs
- Gain a common understanding of the attributes needed to use the model successfully
- Plan for the stages of task development and relationship development
- Develop a common ground as you work through the components and steps of the model

In Part One, I will explain each section of the model and show you how to use it both diagnostically (to see how your partnership is doing) and prescriptively (to show what you can do to improve your partnership).

The model consists of three components:

- Stages of relationship development
- Stages of partnership development
- Past/future orientation environment

Embedded throughout is a system for monitoring the implementation of each component of the model as the partnership and relationship unfold—the Plan–Do–Check–Act (PDCA) cycle.

At either end of the spectrum are the extremes of future and past orientation. Although partnerships in real life can flow in either direction, we want to encourage growth for the future. Characteristics such as whether an organization's culture is open or closed are tied to its past or future orientation. It is within the past or future orientation—the paradigm of the environment in which the partnership exists—that partnering intelligence and all the supporting attributes are used to create the kind of atmosphere the partnership will thrive in. This is a critical point. Think of how the human body flourishes in Earth's atmosphere. The warmth of the sun keeps our bodies comfortable; the rich air nourishes us with oxygen. Now consider, for a moment, your body transported to Mars. If you were left unprotected, how well would you survive? At the moment you arrived, you'd immediately lack oxygen to breathe, and within minutes the frigid Martian atmosphere would freeze your body stiff. Such an environment is deadly to human life. On Earth we are not generally conscious of the environment. We take it for granted as we live out our lives in its invisible blanket. But it is there, protecting, supporting, and nurturing our lives. And the same holds true in partnerships. The atmosphere we create in our partnerships will determine how well we survive. The six attributes that we need to ensure successful partnering create this atmosphere. These six attributes are past/future orientation in decision making, comfort with change, win-win orientation in conflict and problem-solving resolutions, comfort with interdependence, ability to trust, and self-disclosure and feedback.

The two sides of the model present parallel stages of development. On one side are the tasks that define the evolution of the partnership: the stages of partnership development. On the other side are the stages of relationship development. These stages define the natural progression that people and groups go through as they develop and grow. These stages are as predictable as they are fluid. This means that while you can predict they will occur within a period of time, they are easily influenced by outside forces that can cause them to change and even revert to previous stages.

These three major components—past/future orientation environment, stages of partnership development, and stages of relationship development—will help you succeed by showing you how partnerships work best. This plan gives you the tools to evaluate your relationships and pinpoint where to make changes. The best blueprint, however, is only as good as the user. For the Partnership Continuum to be successful, you'll need the skills to read the blueprint and then implement it. For this reason, I'll be going into great detail about the six attributes that make up your partnering intelligence. Along the way you'll find all the surveys and tools you'll need to help you assess and increase your PQ.

THE ESSENCE OF PARTNERSHIPS

There is a saying inscribed on a plaque that hangs in my office: The better I get, the better we get. I love the sentiment behind those words. For me it captures the essence of partnership. Partnership is about helping you get what you want. And the better you know what you want, the better your partners can help you achieve it.

All partnerships start with the individual. Before there are two there is one. You need to know what you want from the partnership before you can ask for it. You need to understand the attributes that make partnerships great before you can expect others to be great partners. The first step, covered here in Chapter 1, is to become aware of the concept of partnering intelligence—to understand that such a thing exists and that it can be increased. In Chapter 2, you'll take the next step by becoming aware of your own PQ.

CHAPTER TWO

Know Thyself

What Is Your PQ?

How good a partner are you? One way to answer this question is to ask yourself another question: How successful are my partnerships? Are you getting everything you expected from them? Have you ever wondered what you could do to improve your partnerships?

ASSESSING YOUR PQ

One of the keys to having a good partnership is the ability to be a good partner. While this may sound elementary, it is tougher than it seems. According to Randy McPherson, CEO of CARA Collision, his partnership's success is due to "finding the right partner with the right skills and the right vision." What are the right skills for being in a partnership? What are the roles and responsibilities of a good partner? These are important questions because all good partnerships start with the individual. If I want a good partnership, then I need to know how to be a good partner.

The genesis of every partnership is a need that has to be fulfilled. Whether in our personal life or in business, we turn to others when we have a need and must enlist the aid of another to get it satisfied. Thus it's up to us to understand what we need from the partnership. If two businesses come together in a partnership, what does each offer the other as a basis for the alliance? For a typical example we can turn to the automotive and car rental businesses. Automobile manufacturers need customers to buy cars; car rental businesses need a source of automobiles that are inexpensive and reliable. As a result of these needs, Avis partners with General Motors to provide itself with a fleet of cars at a reduced rate. Hertz partners with Ford in a similar manner. Each has a need and each gets it met in the form of a partnership. While this may sound like common business sense, how the partnership actually operates depends on the partnering skills of the people involved in managing it. Although the partnership may appear to be between faceless corporations, it is *people* that form and manage partnerships. They are the ones who must have the skills and attributes—the partnering intelligence—to create a successful business relationship.

A high partnering quotient, or PQ, involves certain traits and skills. The traits and skills that lead to successful partnerships include:

- Looks to the future with a clear vision
- Welcomes change
- Creatively resolves conflicts and solves problems
- Values interdependence
- Creates trust through actions and words
- Openly self-discloses information and gives feedback

The following "low PQ" characteristics can doom a partnership to failure:

- Relies on past history for decision making
- Maintains status quo while resisting change
- Desires to win conflicts
- Values independence
- Has low trust of others
- Keeps information to self

There is no secret formula to help you succeed in every partnership you engage in. Each partnership is as unique as the people who make it up. Even so, there are certain characteristics that all successful partnerships have in common: The people in the partnership have a keen sense of self. They understand their own strengths and weaknesses. And they know what they want out of the partnership.

Survey 1 is an assessment tool to help you determine your relative PQ at this moment in time. For unlike your IQ, which changes little during the course of a lifetime, your PQ is a learned intelligence and can change and grow over time. While the PQ Assessment has predictive value—that is, it can identify potential strengths and weaknesses—its primary purpose is to help you increase your self-awareness. It reflects how you perceive yourself in the six attributes of partnering intelligence.

Survey 1
PQ Assessment

Instructions

- **The PQ Assessment is not a test.** There are no right or wrong answers. You cannot pass or fail. It is a self-assessment that poses statements you might not normally think about and asks you to rank each statement.

- **Rank each statement.** The ranking you give should be based on your own perception of the statement and should reflect how you would react in a normal situation. The purpose is not to judge you but to provide you with insights into how you see yourself.

- **Choose a context before responding.** Some people say they behave differently at work than at home or with good friends. If you think your behavior depends on the situation, choose a context (such as your work environment or your home life) and think of that context when responding to all the statements.

- **Do not ponder too long over a statement.** It is best to go with your first reaction. If you contemplate too long, you may begin to second-guess yourself. Your initial reaction is usually your normal response.

- **The results are for your eyes only.** There is no need to show the results to anyone unless you want to.

- **Be as honest as you can.** The more open you are in your responses, the more accurately the PQ Assessment will reflect your true partnering intelligence.

Survey 1	(1) Strongly Agree ⟶ (6) Strongly Disagree
	Circle One
1. I believe a person's basic behavior stays the same over time.	1　2　3　4　5　6
2. I like to do familiar tasks.	1　2　3　4　5　6
3. People tell me I'm inclined to be a competitive person.	1　2　3　4　5　6
4. When I'm with other people, I always make sure my needs are met first.	1　2　3　4　5　6
5. In general, I like it when everyone follows the rules.	1　2　3　4　5　6
6. I like to depend on myself to get things done.	1　2　3　4　5　6
7. People need to prove I can trust them.	1　2　3　4　5　6
8. I feel uncomfortable sharing my feelings with others.	1　2　3　4　5　6
9. I believe that actions speak louder than words.	1　2　3　4　5　6
10. I get frustrated being on a team.	1　2　3　4　5　6
11. I tend to make decisions about someone based on what he or she has done before.	1　2　3　4　5　6
12. I feel very anxious when I'm in a new situation.	1　2　3　4　5　6
13. If I don't win a conflict, I feel upset.	1　2　3　4　5　6
14. When I need to go somewhere, I prefer to depend on myself to get there.	1　2　3　4　5　6
15. I like to have people prove their facts.	1　2　3　4　5　6
16. I believe in keeping my personal life to myself.	1　2　3　4　5　6

Survey 1 continued	(1) Strongly Agree ➝ (6) Strongly Disagree
	Circle One

	1	2	3	4	5	6
17. Past history is a better predictor of events than a future plan.	1	2	3	4	5	6
18. I get very nervous when I meet new people.	1	2	3	4	5	6
19. I prefer to use techniques I've used before to accomplish new tasks.	1	2	3	4	5	6
20. I'd rather give in to another's wishes than argue for my point.	1	2	3	4	5	6
21. I rarely share family information with others.	1	2	3	4	5	6
22. I think it's important to check up on people to make sure they do what they say they'll do.	1	2	3	4	5	6
23. I will give up something important to reach a compromise.	1	2	3	4	5	6
24. I get upset when people tell me something about myself I don't like.	1	2	3	4	5	6
25. I am more interested in actuality than I am in possibilities.	1	2	3	4	5	6
26. I prefer a signed contract to a handshake.	1	2	3	4	5	6
27. I like having my day planned and scheduled and get frustrated when I have to change it.	1	2	3	4	5	6
28. I feel I am more of a private person than one who is outgoing.	1	2	3	4	5	6
29. I would rather be by myself than spend time with other people.	1	2	3	4	5	6
30. In an argument, being right is more important than maintaining the other's dignity.	1	2	3	4	5	6

Scoring the Survey

To score the survey you'll need to calculate the number of points you received for each statement. To do this, look at each statement. Now fill out the following worksheet and add up your total points. The lowest possible score is 30; the highest is 180.

Statement	Points	Statement	Points
1		16	
2		17	
3		18	
4		19	
5		20	
6		21	
7		22	
8		23	
9		24	
10		25	
11		26	
12		27	
13		28	
14		29	
15		30	
		Total Score	

30–80 points: You have identified yourself as someone with a low PQ.

81–130 points: You have identified yourself as someone with a medium PQ.

131–180 points: You have identified yourself as someone with a high PQ.

Your ranking reflects how you view yourself at this moment in time. There is no right or wrong, no good or bad. You need to determine for yourself if this score accurately reflects the status of your partnering skills today.

Interpreting the Results

The PQ Assessment (Survey 1) ranks the specific attributes that measure your partnering intelligence. These attributes are critical for building successful partnerships. Each statement supports a primary attribute and may reflect one or more secondary attributes needed for a high PQ and successful use of the Partnership Continuum model. The six attributes the assessment measures are:

- Past/future orientation in decision making
- Comfort with change
- Win-win orientation
- Comfort with interdependence
- Ability to trust
- Self-disclosure and feedback

The PQ Assessment can be used to predict which attributes you may have trouble bringing to a partnership. For example, if you ranked low on the statements regarding comfort with change, you may have difficulty with the changes partnerships inevitably create. The assessment can also help you diagnose which attributes you might want to consider strengthening. If trust seems to be an issue in your partnership and you scored low in trust, for instance, you might want to examine your ability to give and receive trust. In Chapter 8 you can learn how to analyze your results on each of the six attributes.

Each of the thirty statements reflects one attribute. However, because of the systemic nature of partnering and the intelligence that is needed to accomplish it successfully, no single attribute stands alone. If you have a low ability to trust, for instance, you may have difficulty creating win-win conflict resolution because you may not believe your partner will uphold his or her end of the agreement. Now let's examine the statements one by one.

1.   I believe a person's basic behavior stays the same over time.

Attribute: Past/future orientation

Interpretation: This statement speculates on how you view people and their expected behavior. If you believe that people's behavior doesn't change over time, then you probably rely on past history to make decisions about people. This may also reflect your desire to maintain the status quo. It's more comfortable to judge people as "you have always known them" than to risk changing your view of them and being proved wrong.

If you ranked this statement low, you may want to:

- Review how you make decisions about people. Take Survey 4, Past vs. Future Orientation, in Chapter 9.

- Think about your willingness to change your perceptions of people.

2.   I like to do familiar tasks.

Attribute: Comfort with change

Interpretation: Maintaining the status quo means you like things just as they are and do not welcome change. People who like to do familiar tasks learn how to do something and then enjoy doing it over and over. Change often causes them anxiety and makes them uneasy. In partnerships, we are frequently asked to do something differently. If change makes you uncomfortable, you may find a partnership an anxiety-ridden affair.

If you ranked this statement low, you may want to:

- Examine how you manage change in your relationships and tasks. Review the information in Chapter 10 regarding change, then do Exercise 8, Partnership Stressors, in Chapter 10.

3.   People tell me I'm inclined to be a competitive person.

Attribute: Win-win orientation

Interpretation: Competitively driven people focus on creating situations where they can win. While sometimes this helps them succeed, it can be a liability when forming a partnership. In partnerships, the focus switches from a competitive win-lose dynamic to a collaborative win-win approach. To get everyone's needs met, all parties must work together. Competitiveness, by its very nature, sets up win-lose dynamics and impedes the growth of healthy partnerships. Competitive behavior is also an indicator of a high need for independence. The nature of competition means you "go it alone" to win.

If you ranked this statement low, you may want to:

- Determine your conflict resolution style (see Chapter 11).
- Investigate your willingness to rely on another to get your needs met. Take Survey 6, Independent or Interdependent?, in Chapter 12.

4. *When I'm with other people, I always make sure my needs are met first.*

   Attribute: Comfort with interdependence

Interpretation: The statement implies discomfort with feeling dependent on another to get your needs met. Focusing on getting your needs met first makes you less dependent on others. This demonstrates an independent attitude. It may also reveal a lack of trust that others will help you get your needs met. You feel you need to fend for yourself. This statement also reflects a desire to ensure that your personal needs get met in a group setting. By wanting to get your needs met first, there is an inference of a win-lose conflict resolution style—that is, "I'll get mine and we'll worry about the others later."

If you ranked this statement low, you may want to:

- Investigate your ability to depend on others to get your needs met.
- Talk to your partner about the level of trust you have in your partnership. Take Survey 7, the Personal Trust Questionnaire, in Chapter 13.
- Examine your conflict resolution style (see Chapter 11).

5. *In general, I like it when everyone follows the rules.*

   Attribute: Comfort with change

Interpretation: This statement touches on your ability to risk the unknown. When people follow the rules, there is a predictability that, for some, creates comfort. Predictability reduces risk. When things are predictable, we trust that everything will turn out the way it always has in the past. Consequently, this statement speculates that when we follow the rules, we maintain the status quo. And when we maintain the status quo, we know the outcome and don't have to worry about it. In effect, we trust the outcome will meet our needs and expectations.

If you ranked this statement low, you may want to:

- Think about your willingness to change. Do Exercise 8, Partnership Stressors, in Chapter 10 to identify areas where you want to develop strategies for change.
- Examine the level of trust you have in others.

6.   *I like to depend on myself to get things done.*

Attribute: Comfort with interdependence

Interpretation: This statement deals with your level of comfort when depending on someone else. When we'd rather do tasks ourselves, it's often a sign that we don't want to depend on someone else to help us. We may fear the job won't get done or that we'll be disappointed with the finished product. It's just plain easier to do it ourselves. It may also indicate that we have a certain way of doing something and don't wish to deviate from our routine.

If you ranked this statement low, you may want to:

- Examine your comfort level with depending on others. Review Survey 6, Independent or Interdependent?, in Chapter 12.
- Reflect on your ability to change how you accomplish a task.

7.   *People need to prove I can trust them.*

Attribute: Ability to trust

Interpretation: Some people trust freely. Others need to build trust. Some never learn to trust at all. If people need to constantly "prove" themselves to you, then you probably have low trust. This may also mean you make decisions about people based on what they've demonstrated to you in the past. If they've disappointed you, you'll continue to have low expectations and trust.

If you ranked this statement low, you may want to:

- Think about your ability to trust. Focus on Chapter 13 to determine your level of trust with others.
- Reflect on your decision-making style.

8. I feel uncomfortable sharing my feelings with others.

Attribute: Self-disclosure and feedback

Interpretation: The ability to disclose information about oneself creates two important dynamics for successful partnerships. First, self-disclosure creates a sense of openness between the partners. This enables each partner to communicate important information about his or her needs and provides opportunities to give feedback. Second, self-disclosure is a trust-building device that creates a powerful bond, moving the partnership toward its objectives.

If you ranked this statement low, you may want to:

- Focus on your ability to reveal information about yourself to others. Review the information in Chapter 14.
- Do Exercise 11, the Self-Disclosure Assessment, in Chapter 14.
- Examine your ability to trust others with information about yourself.

9. I believe that actions speak louder than words.

Attribute: Ability to trust

Interpretation: If you don't believe that someone will do as he or she says, then there is low trust between the parties. People consistently doing what they've promised builds trust. This may also reflect people's ability to be open about their true intentions. If a person says one thing but does another, he or she may not have felt enough trust to openly disclose underlying intentions. In other words, the environment of the partnership does not support building trust and creating openness. And, if you can't take a person at his or her word, then you're probably basing that decision on an event in the past when you were disappointed. This may indicate that your decision-making style is based on past history.

If you ranked this statement low, you may want to:

- Consider what part you play in people's ability to talk about their true intentions and be open to helping them meet their needs.
- Look at the reasons you have low trust. Take Survey 9, the Partners Trust Questionnaire, in Chapter 13 to develop expectations between you and your partner.
- Review how you make decisions about people.

10. I get frustrated being on a team.

Attribute: Comfort with interdependence

Interpretation: When people have a strong sense of independence, teamwork is painful for them. They feel dependent on others to achieve their goals and don't feel in control of the situation. And if these goals are not achieved, they are disappointed and may blame their partners. Often they'd rather work by themselves since they trust the job will get done that way.

If you ranked this statement low, you may want to:

- Examine your need for independence.
- Determine why you don't trust others to help you accomplish your goals.

11. I tend to make decisions about someone based on what he or she has done before.

Attribute: Past/future orientation

Interpretation: This statement is designed to elicit how you make decisions about your interactions with people. If you make a decision based on a past event, you have a past orientation. But if you judge each individual based on the agreements you've made and then determine how well that person lived up to the agreements, you have a future orientation. This statement may also reflect your comfort with change ("so and so always does this") and your ability to trust that people can change and live up to their agreements with you.

If you ranked this statement low, you may want to:

- Review how you make decisions about people.
- Think about your willingness to change your perceptions of others.

12. *I feel very anxious when I'm in a new situation.*

Attribute: Comfort with change

Interpretation: This statement speculates on your level of comfort with new situations. People who are uncomfortable in new situations are usually uncomfortable with change. Change takes such people out of their comfort zone and creates anxiety. This statement may also reflect a need to maintain the status quo.

If you ranked this statement low, you may want to:

- Review your level of comfort with change and think about how you might manage change in a way that produces less anxiety for you.
- Think about your need to maintain the status quo (your past orientation decision-making style).

13. *If I don't win a conflict, I feel upset.*

Attribute: Win-win orientation

Interpretation: Competitive people need to win conflicts. If they don't, they feel bad. But your partnering intelligence increases when you're able to create a win-win resolution within your partnership. This statement may also reflect a past orientation. When competitive people win a conflict, they feel they can control the situation and are not required to build a mutually agreeable plan.

If you ranked this statement low, you may want to:

- Review your conflict resolution style and think about how you can move toward more collaborative resolutions.
- Think about your level of comfort with change.
- Determine if you have a past orientation decision-making style.

14. *When I need to go somewhere, I prefer to depend on myself to get there.*

Attribute: Comfort with interdependence

Interpretation: This statement provides insight into your feelings about depending on other people. There are those of us who must drive ourselves everywhere and those who are willing to share the ride. If you are comfortable depending on another, you are comfortable making arrangements for others to provide you with transportation. But fiercely independent people, regardless of the transportation options available, feel compelled to provide their own mode of transport—one they can "depend" on. This statement also reflects your comfort with change, since depending on another may include a change in plans. It also touches on your ability to trust since you must trust that another will do what he or she says when you make such an arrangement.

If you ranked this statement low, you may want to:

- Review your level of dependence. Are you so independent that you can't allow yourself to get a basic need such as transportation met?
- Think about your comfort with change
- Think about your level of trust in others.

15. *I like to have people prove their facts.*

Attribute: Ability to trust

Interpretation: When there is low trust, people demand proof. While this is not inherently a bad thing, if you're unable to believe someone without examining the facts, this demonstrates an inability to trust. In relationships, a person's feelings and perceptions are his or her facts. When business partnerships achieve quantum improvements, many decisions are based on intuitive knowledge and feelings. How are you going to prove the facts in these situations? Partnerships need unconditional trust, which frees people up to take risks and move into the creative zone without restrictions. Businesses that have the foresight and courage to develop this kind of trust within their partnerships are the ones that will succeed. This statement may also reflect your comfort with change. If you demand to see the "facts," you may not be willing to change without extensive reasons for changing. And this may indicate discomfort with change.

If you ranked this statement low, you may want to:

- Examine ways you can improve your ability to trust others. Talk to your partners about what trust means to you. Ask them to tell you what trust means to them. Use Survey 8, the Partners Trust Questionnaire, in Chapter 13.

- Think about your level of comfort with change.

16. I believe in keeping my personal life to myself.

Attribute: Self-disclosure and feedback

Interpretation: We are the same people at work that we are at home. And while we may alter the façade, our core values do not change. This statement indicates reluctance to disclose parts of our personal life to others. If we hide a part of ourselves from others, people sense we are not being fully genuine. Humans have a sixth sense when they think someone is not sharing information with them. This starts a cycle of mistrust between people: If you don't share something with me, then I'm not going to share something with you. And so the cycle begins.

If you ranked this statement low, you may want to:

- Review your ability to self-disclose. You may want to go over the process of self-disclosure with a close friend or loved one.

- Think about your willingness to change your perceptions of others.

17. Past history is a better predictor of events than a future plan.

Attribute: Past/future orientation

Interpretation: While it's true that we can learn a lot from history, to make decisions based solely on historic data would be a mistake. People, events, and partnerships *change.* I use the analogy of driving a car while looking in the rearview mirror. It may be useful to see where you've been, but it's more important to know where you're going. If you believe that past history is a better predictor than a future plan, you may have a past orientation. You may also feel uncomfortable with change and therefore prefer to maintain the status quo.

If you ranked this statement low, you may want to:

- Review how you make decisions about people and events.
- Think about your willingness to change your perceptions of people and their behavior.
- Consider your level of comfort with change.

18. I get very nervous when I meet new people.

Attribute: Comfort with change

Interpretation: While meeting people for the first time can sometimes create mild anxiety for people, getting very nervous may indicate that you have a problem with change. New people bring new and often unexpected challenges. If you are uncomfortable dealing with change, meeting new people may heighten your anxiety. This may be true for you in partnerships as well.

If you ranked this statement low, you may want to:

- Think about what makes you uncomfortable in meeting new people.
- Develop a plan for helping you increase your comfort with change (Chapter 10).

19. I prefer to use techniques I've used before to accomplish new tasks.

Attribute: Past/future orientation

Interpretation: If you prefer to use the same techniques on each task, you may end up making the same mistakes over and over. This may indicate that you're comfortable with the status quo and are unwilling to try something new. People with a past orientation rely on the status quo to resolve new issues—and often find themselves repeatedly confronted with the same problems. This may also reflect your level of comfort with change. The two dynamics often collude to create a reinforcing mechanism that is hard for people to break.

If you ranked this statement low, you may want to:

- Review how you make decisions about tasks.
- Think about your level of comfort with change.

20. I'd rather give in to another's wishes than argue for my ↲

Attribute: Win-win orientation

Interpretation: When a person is always accommodating another's wishes, resentment builds up. And when this resentment reaches a critical stage, the accommodator begins to act out the resentment. In most cases, this plays out in passive-aggressive behavior. That is, people will act passively toward their partner and then aggressively work to undermine whatever event they accommodated. This type of sabotage is a sure partnership killer.

If you ranked this statement low, you may want to:

- Review Chapter 11 to determine your conflict resolution style.
- Consider strategies to move you to win-win solutions.

21. I rarely share family information with others.

Attribute: Self-disclosure and feedback

Interpretation: People who tend to keep personal information strictly personal are often uncomfortable with self-disclosure. While we all have boundaries between our personal and business lives, it's normal to talk about your spouse, loved ones, children, and outside activities. People who are so closed that they cannot share family information send a nonverbal message to others. That message is generally perceived as mistrust and a lack of candor. People respond to this message by shutting down communication themselves. Ultimately this will hurt the partnership.

If you ranked this statement low, you may want to:

- Read Chapter 14 and consider how the JoHari Window might affect your relations in the partnership. The more we disclose, the more we are able to build trust.
- Review Survey 7, the Personal Trust Questionnaire, in Chapter 13. Closely linked with self-disclosure is the ability to trust. If you don't trust people you won't feel comfortable with self-disclosure.

22. I think it's important to check up on people to make sure they do what they say they'll do.

Attribute: Ability to trust

Interpretation: This statement reflects your ability to trust that your partners will do what they promise. Trust is built incrementally over time. People say they will do something and then they do it. The more often this occurs, the higher the trust level. But when we don't trust them to do what they say, we feel compelled to "check up on them." This statement might also reveal a past orientation. If we've had a bitter experience and have low trust, we begin to expect to be let down by everyone. We need to think about how we can begin to expect people to live up to their agreements.

If you ranked this statement low, you may want to:

- Sit down with a partner and take Survey 8, the Partners Trust Questionnaire, in Chapter 13.
- Review the information in Chapter 9 to determine what you might do to move from a past to a future orientation.

23. I will give up something important to reach a compromise.

Attribute: Win-win orientation

Interpretation: Compromise sets up a lose-lose dynamic. If you're willing to give up something of value, ultimately it will come back to haunt you. This is because it's important to you. I call compromise lose-lose because both parties lose the energy to resolve the conflict in a collaborative way that will end it. Rather than giving in to the compromise, partners should try to figure out how to use the energy to create a new solution in which both partners win.

If you ranked this statement low, you may want to:

- Review your conflict resolution style.
- Review the strategies and outcomes of different conflict resolution styles in Chapter 11.

24. I get upset when people tell me something about myself I don't like.

Attribute: Self-disclosure and feedback

Interpretation: When we hear comments about ourselves that we don't like, it often means that they have hit a nerve. We may see the trait being described but adamantly deny it. The ability to accept feedback is closely associated with self-disclosure. Remember, feedback reflects as much on the giver as it does on the receiver. Be open to the feedback. And then see if others provide you with similar comments.

If you ranked this statement low, you may want to:
- Think about the process of receiving and giving feedback. You may want to review Chapter 14 on self-disclosure and feedback.
- Do Exercise 12, the Feedback Assessment, and review Exercise 13, the Feedback Observation Checklist, in Chapter 14.

25. I am more interested in actuality than I am in possibilities

Attribute: Past/future orientation

Interpretation: People who prefer to deal with actuality rather than possibilities may be uncomfortable making decisions based on the unknown. If this is an issue for you, it may reflect a past orientation in your decision-making style; that is, you are more comfortable making decisions and plans based on the here and now than on the future. You may also feel some discomfort with change. Current reality is tangible and many people have a sense of control over it. Since the future is unknown, and change may be required, possibilities may cause anxiety over what changes they will bring.

If you ranked this statement low, you may want to:
- Review how you make decisions about people using a past orientation.
- Take the Past/Future Orientation Inventory in Chapter 9.
- Examine how you manage change in your life. Review the information in Chapter 10.

26. I prefer a signed contract to a handshake.

Attribute: Ability to trust

Interpretation: If you have negotiated your partnership with openness and honesty and using self-disclosure and feedback, by the time the negotiations are completed a handshake should be sufficient to seal the agreement. If you need the security of a signed legal document, this may be an indication that you do not trust your partner. If you need to bring in the lawyers during the early stages of partnership development, you need to think about whether you truly trust this partner.

If you ranked this statement low, you may want to:

- Think about your ability to trust. Why do you need to have a signed contract to feel secure in what you have negotiated?
- Focus on Chapter 13 and take the Partners' Trust Questionnaire.

27. *I like having my day planned and scheduled and get frustrated when I have to change it.*

Attribute: Comfort with change

Interpretation: Schedule changes and flexibility are the norm for most of us. If schedule changes make you feel frustrated and anxious, you may want to think about why these changes bother you so much. Partnerships are full of uncertainties and change, and if this is difficult for you, you may have a problem being in partnership with someone.

If you ranked this statement low, you may want to:

- Review your level of comfort with change and think about how you might manage change in a way that will produce less anxiety for you.
- Review the information in Chapter 10.

28. *I feel I am more of a private person than one who is outgoing.*

Attribute: Self-disclosure and feedback

Interpretation: If you feel that you are basically a private person, you may be sending signals to partners that you are uncomfortable disclosing information about yourself or your needs. While it may be that you are simply introverted, your ability to self-disclose to your partner is crucial if trust is to be established. Early on you may want to address your personal preference or personality style with partners to ensure that there will be no misunderstanding.

If you ranked this statement low, you may want to:

- Review the information in Chapter 14.
- Review the JoHari model for communication between you and your partner.

- Learn more about yourself by taking a personality inventory, such as the *Myers-Briggs Type Indicator®*.
- Review Chapter 13 on the ability to trust. People sometimes refuse to self-disclose information when they feel low trust.

29. I would rather be by myself than spend time with other people.

Attribute: Comfort with interdependence

Interpretation: People who prefer to spend time by themselves are generally introverted in their personality preference. While this in itself is neither good nor bad, if one becomes too reclusive, it makes it difficult for them to depend on anyone for anything. Even highly introverted people need to interact with others to help get their needs met. If you are uncomfortable being with others, you may be sending your partners mixed and confusing messages. You may also want to think about your ability to trust. Do you avoid being with people because you do not trust them enough to get to know you?

If you ranked this statement low, you may want to:

- Explore the reason you prefer to be alone. Are you recharging your personal energy, or is something else going on for you?
- Review your ability to trust others. Take the My Personal Trust Questionnaire in Chapter 13.

30. In an argument, being right is more important than maintaining the other's dignity.

Attribute: Win-win orientation

Interpretation: If it is so important that you be right in an argument that you would hurt another person's dignity, then you are probably not using a win-win style of conflict resolution. It is important when resolving conflicts to be sure our partners feel that they also have won. Being right is not more important than affording another human being the respect and dignity he or she deserves.

If you ranked this statement low, you may want to:

- Review your conflict resolution style.
- Read Chapter 11. Then review the guidelines for achieving consensus in decision making.

TAKING THE NEXT STEP

By now you are starting to get a feel for your partnering intelligence. By taking Survey 1, the PQ Assessment, you've already taken a big step toward increasing your PQ—you've increased your self-awareness by figuring out your relative PQ. Do you have a high, medium, or low PQ? Remember: You can *learn* partnering intelligence. You now have some insight into the attributes that compose it. And now that you are aware of your PQ, you can begin to improve it.

Successful partnering is unique in that you have a major influence over the outcome of the partnership but can control only your part. The more intelligent the individual partners become, the better the partnership gets. This intelligence increases exponentially when the partners use a logical process for creating and developing the partnership. The process—the Partnership Continuum—is the subject of Part One.

PART TWO

The Partnership Continuum

A Model for Increasing Your PQ

You have now had an opportunity to assess your current PQ and have gained some insight into the attributes that are required to be a good partner. Now you are ready to put this knowledge to work. It's time to make a leap—a leap from the individual to the partnership. For most of us, the first partnerships we encounter in business settings are internal partnerships. Often our success is measured by our ability to work as a member of a team to accomplish a task. For others, however, partnerships are focused on expanding business opportunities and creating strategic alliances with other businesses. In both situations, the process is the same. Whether we're focused on managing an internal team or an external business alliance, the model, the process, and the skills are the same. Regardless of the focus, partnerships are alliances between people. And it is how people interact with each other that determines the success or failure of a partnership.

So the question becomes: How do you use the Partnership Continuum model to take the quantum leap, increase your partnering intelligence, and build a successful partnership? Part Two explains how to utilize the model to help you manage your partnerships. The Partnership Continuum is a thoughtful, organized approach that balances the task and relationship aspects of a partnership. Once you understand the components and attributes that make up successful partnerships, you can discuss the Partnership Continuum with your partners at work. While explaining the model, you will be creating an opportunity to talk with your peers, your bosses, and/or your employees about a disciplined approach for building partnerships. Partnerships are too important to be allowed to evolve by happenstance. After the groundwork of the process has been laid, you can begin to discuss the various attributes that ensure its success. You will have begun to create a common foundation on which you can build. This is especially true for those who wish to form external partnerships. The model provides the context and the language for discussing how you want the partnership to develop and gives potential partners a step-by-step guide to success.

By using the Partnership Continuum model as a blueprint, you will be expanding your partnering intelligence beyond yourself. You will be including your partners in the process. By doing this, you will not only increase your own PQ but will help your partners increase theirs as well, bringing even greater potential for success.

CHAPTER THREE

Overview of the Partnership Continuum

Blueprint for Successful Partnerships

My approach to forming and maintaining healthy, successful, and mutually beneficial partnerships is based on a process. By *process* I mean a deliberate, planned operation. After discussing the stages that make up the process, we can understand the various relationships between these stages and the specific influence each stage brings to bear on the whole process and its outcome. This is the reason we need to approach partnerships from a holistic perspective. Partnerships are systems, not simply parts. You do not expect the human body to function properly if you remove a piece of the "human system"—the heart, for instance. Since partnerships are systems, too, you cannot expect a partnership to function if you ignore one of its components. You can't just work on the task and ignore the relationship and expect a successful outcome.

In the Partnership Continuum model (see Figure 2), I present these stages as sequential steps to take, as in "how to bake a cake." The Partnership Continuum is the recipe for a successful partnership. We can describe the process developmentally—as in "after this happens, this can happen." In the process of making an automobile, for example,

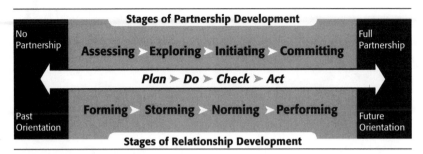

Figure 2 The Partnership Continuum Model

the design and modeling stage precedes the assembly stage. I use a four-stage model to describe how healthy, mutually satisfying relationships develop. I know that some relationships never get to the later stages because they fail to develop properly in an earlier stage. This, of course, puts more emphasis on the earlier stages. Once the partners have spent sufficient time together, the later stages occur more naturally and require less adherence to specific activities because trust between the partners has been established. And this trust permits the partnership to take more risks in accomplishing its goals.

The Partnership Continuum model guides us through the incremental stages involved in creating successful partnerships. As Figure 2 shows, the model has three components:

• Stages of relationship development

• Stages of partnership development

• Past/future orientation environment

In this chapter I'll walk you through each stage of the Partnership Continuum model. As we go through each stage, I'll describe what you can expect when the partnership is at that stage. I'll talk about the stages of relationship development and explain the types of behaviors you can expect to see. I'll talk about the stages of partnership development and the activities that need to occur. Then I'll explain the crucial distinction between an environment with a past orientation and one with a future orientation. In sum, then, this chapter will help you move through the Partnership Continuum model quickly and begin reaping the benefits of the partnership. Let's begin with the stages of relationship development.

STAGES OF RELATIONSHIP DEVELOPMENT

Forming ➤ *Storming* ➤ *Norming* ➤ *Performing*

Every person and every group moves through four stages in the process of attaining a long-lasting relationship based on mutual benefit, trust, and respect. That individuals and groups go through this predictable cycle of forming, storming, norming, and performing as they develop relationships was illustrated for me early in my consulting career. I've seen this cycle occur quickly or last for months, depending on the relations within the group and its need to be together.

When a relationship is in the *forming* stage, people are generally polite to each other. Most are reserved and allow a group leader or dominant individual to control activities. Others may not reveal much about themselves or disclose their reasons for being involved in the group. They sit back and take a wait-and-see attitude. The important lesson is this: Investing time and energy in clarifying objectives and expressing our needs in the forming stage has a positive influence on the development of the relationship.

The forming stage is the optimum time to clarify the issues and dynamics of the relationship. During the forming stage of development, most of us have questions that need to be addressed—questions about roles, rules, procedures, and the partnership agenda. "What are we doing?" is a question frequently heard in the forming stage. During this period people are also asking themselves how much they want to invest. They are struggling to understand whether they are "in or out"—and if they are "in," what is the price of admission? Consequently, the forming stage needs a strong leader to give direction and set the tone of the partnership until trust is established and situational leadership can emerge in a natural way.

These issues, if not addressed up front, will resurface later and can sabotage the development of trust. Some partners are so eager to "do the deal" that they forget they're interacting with other people who have their own needs and wants. Impatience at the forming stage is a signal of a potential "one-night stand relationship."

Next the relationship moves into the *storming* stage. Here a clash of ideas and behavior creates the conditions for conflict. Some of the initial politeness may begin to give way to more assertive behavior. Conflict begins to erupt between individuals or group members. Individuals begin to challenge the leadership of the dominant person. People begin to assert themselves and test the limits of the relationship. They also want to see how much trust has been established. The better the relationship created in the forming stage, the easier it is to deal with conflict in the storming stage. Though most people dislike conflict, the storming stage is a sign of growth in the development of the relationship. In this stage, people assert what is important for them to continue in the relationship. The group establishes boundaries; individuals express their needs; and, with luck, the relationship develops.

The *norming* stage occurs when those in the relationship have identified their own needs. Having aligned their needs with the goals of the partnership, now they are able to contribute to the overall success of the endeavor. The people in the relationship establish acceptable verbal and nonverbal behavior. They clarify values that govern behavior in the relationship. People start to know what is expected of them. Roles are established and defined.

People migrate to their roles in a normal and natural way. They feel confident of what is expected of them. Collaboration—rather than confrontation or avoidance—resolves conflict. People feel comfortable with each other and begin to enjoy the personal relationships they've established in the partnership. They start to have fun. They experiment and try new and daring activities as they deepen the level of trust they feel with each other.

Norming occurs when people see their personal success tied to the success of the partnership. By the time the relationship reaches the norming stage, the values and norms of behavior have been integrated into the culture of the partnership. The relationship then moves into the *performing* stage. In this stage, creative energies surface, increase, and flow abundantly as partners generate synergy. Now people perform at highly creative, efficient, and productive levels. The partnership achieves goals that often exceed expectations at the outset.

Responding to Changes

But nothing in life is cut and dried. People move back and forth between stages as the dynamics of the relationship change. Relationships move between stages in response to outside forces and influences (see Figure 3).

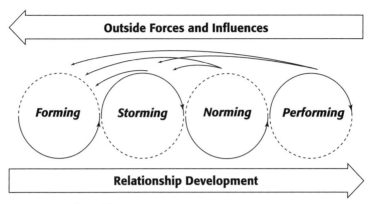

Figure 3   Impact of Outside Forces

Without interference, the stages of relationship development flow in the direction shown. But when outside forces intervene, a group may revert to a previous stage. When new members are added, for example, the group often reverts to the forming stage.

For instance, a group of people representing different departments in the same organization may have joined together in a partnership to address the issue of quality. They've functioned well for months. They are currently in the norming stage of development. Then suddenly the vice president of one department informs the group that the team's objectives have changed. Some members object that this vice president is manipulating the group to focus efforts on improvements for his department at the expense of others. As conflicts arise about the team's former objective versus the new objective, the group reverts temporarily to the storming stage. If the team as a whole can clarify and agree upon new objectives, the group will return to the norming stage. Because the group has already established a level of trust among themselves, they should be able to move forward. Ideally, members will feel confident addressing issues and resolving them in an open manner and with group consensus. Rebounding from norming to storming and back is inherently easier than initially evolving through the storming phase.

The longer a group has been together and the greater the trust among its members, the faster it will return to the highest stage of development it had achieved before the interruption. Groups that return to norming and performing levels despite changes and new challenges are invaluable human assets. Creating partnerships that can function at the higher levels requires work. Because of the time and effort needed to build good partnerships, keeping high-functioning groups together makes sense. Part Two deals with the essential skills that all partnerships require to build healthy relationships. The more skills we can master, the higher we progress on the partnering intelligence scale. And as we learn to be more trustworthy, negotiate better, and communicate more effectively, we become more valuable as potential partners.

Using the Stages

Now that you understand the theory behind the stages of relationship development, I want to show you how to use them as a tool for developing partnerships. Although many people cognitively understand the stages, they promptly forget about them in a group setting. Yet this is when they are needed the most.

First, it pays to talk about them. With some groups I draw a diagram of the stages of relationship development on a large piece of paper. I start the partnership meetings out by asking: "Where are we in our relationship development?" I then ask everyone to make a mark on the scale to indicate where he or she thinks the partnership is in its development. While this may seem elementary, it's a basic technique for generating discussions that strengthen the partnership and move it to the next level of development. It can be used as a tool to pinpoint problem areas that may be preventing the team from moving ahead with the task. At the close of the meeting I do something similar by asking how the meeting went. I always ask that question from two perspectives—that is, from a task perspective and from a relationship perspective. While initially they may be reluctant to disclosing their feelings about the relationship, most people become comfortable with the question and even begin to look forward to discussing how the relationship is developing.

Another way that I check for relationship development is to hand out the Relationship Feedback Assessment (Survey 2) at the start of the meeting. I ask each person to fill out the assessment anonymously and then I post the responses on a large sheet of paper. Based on the feedback from the partners, we develop a plan to continue our progress or alter our course to improve what's wrong. A version of my survey is presented here as an exercise you may copy and use on your own or with your partners.

Survey 2
Relationship Feedback Assessment

Instructions

Read each statement and circle the number or word that comes closest to reflecting your opinion on the relationship between partners.

Relationship Feedback	Never ⟶ Always				
			Circle One		
1. I trust the other partners in this partnership.	1	2	3	4	5
2. I think the other partners trust me.	1	2	3	4	5
3. I am comfortable expressing my ideas in this partnership.	1	2	3	4	5
4. I feel that my needs are being met in this partnership.	1	2	3	4	5
5. I help others in this partnership meet their needs.	1	2	3	4	5
6. I think we are at the_____ stage of relationship development.	forming	storming	norming	performing	

Scoring the Survey

Each person has filled out the Relationship Feedback Assessment, (Survey 2). On a large sheet of paper I list the statements 1 through 6 and draw the corresponding grid or stage of relationship development. I then ask each person to come up and mark where he or she ranked the partnership in terms of its relationship development. After everyone has responded, I average the score for each statement. If the ranking is low for a particular statement, I ask why and let the group talk about the scoring. If a ranking is high, I ask what we need to do to continue to build the relationship development of the partnership. This is an excellent tool to use in opening the discussion of the relationship development of the partnership.

STAGES OF PARTNERSHIP DEVELOPMENT

Assessing ➤ *Exploring* ➤ *Initiating* ➤ *Committing*

We identify our own needs. We find potential partners. We communicate what we want. We act in accordance with our promises and commitments. In the four stages of partnership development we're creating a new future with our partner. Through the accomplishment of tasks, the deepening of trust, and the practice of direct communication, our partnership grows and develops. In theory, there's no doubt the script makes sense. The show should be a hit every time.

In practice, however, we're dealing with people who do things for their own reasons, not according to a script. We need to account for various levels of partnering intelligence, which can change in an instant. Analyzing and understanding the process allows us to manage each stage more intelligently.

Each step that we take during the stages of partnership development presents us with an opportunity to accrue trust in our trust bank. And as our trust account grows, we feel more confident about taking risks. Once we feel secure enough to take chances, the possibilities become boundless. This is when we begin to generate synergy and enter the creative zone. The creative zone is a state of being—a place where we feel totally secure and can let all our synapses spark ideas at once. This is what businesses really want: the creative spark that differentiates them from everyone else.

While there may be many different ways of moving partnerships into the creative zone, I know the Partnership Continuum model works. It is structured enough to provide a framework for those who need it and holistic enough to cover the two critical components of any good partnership: task and relationship. So here are the four stages of partnership development. First, partners must be willing to examine their own readiness, willingness, and ability to engage in the process. Starting with *assessing,* the first stage, enables you to figure out what it is you want from a partnership. It helps you become a more intelligent partner. What's your PQ? Do you know what you expect from a partner? Do you understand your own limitations? Can you make a decision to change your behavior if necessary?

Second, you'll need to communicate with a prospective partner. In this second stage, *exploring* areas of common interest and mutual benefit will balance the partnership at the outset. You'll need to help others become better partners. Once you've identified a potential partner, explained what you need, and helped your potential partner see the benefits to be gained, you can plan a joint project.

Third, you can seize the opportunities to develop trust by agreeing to initial activities. In this third stage, *initiating,* you can work with your partner one step at a time to test and build your partnership. As you gain more trust by demonstrating you can work together effectively, you'll make more commitments and strengthen your partnership. This is the fourth stage, *committing.*

THE PLAN–DO–CHECK–ACT CYCLE

The success of a partnership depends on what is actually accomplished—not on what was intended or possible. As we define our expectations of each other in terms of a task, we also define the expectations in the relationship. We talk about our relationship in terms of the behavior that is acceptable. We also agree in a collaborative spirit to hold each other accountable. This is where the relationship issues involve our personal styles of handling conflict. If you're not happy with the way I'm performing a task, what will you do about it? How will we communicate?

Rather than simply hoping the partnership delivers what it's capable of achieving, I use a structured process that helps me manage the outcomes. This process is called the Plan–Do–Check–Act cycle (or the Shewhart cycle or Deming cycle).

Walter A. Shewhart, a statistician at Bell Telephone Laboratories in New York, developed a technique to reduce process variation in tasks that workers performed. He developed this planning cycle to improve the output of his processes and bring them under what he called "statistical" control. Later Dr. W. Edwards Deming referred to the Shewhart cycle as the Plan–Do–Check–Act cycle. Deming introduced it to the Japanese to help rebuild their economy after World War II. This cycle has been a cornerstone of the Japanese economic miracle ever since the 1960s and is still used today. In fact, the Japanese call it the Deming Cycle of Quality.

The Plan–Do–Check–Act cycle is as useful in developing relationships as it is in managing statistical control or performing a task. I use this simple tool repeatedly throughout the Partnership Continuum model. Now let us turn to a more comprehensive exploration of the cycle.

Step 1: Plan

 The first step is to decide what actions we should take to accomplish a task. Breaking down a manufacturing or sales process or a performance procedure into its parts is not hard to do. We also need to plan our relationship. We need to single out the components of the relationship that we agree are important: the nature of the relationship and how we'll resolve conflicts, make decisions, and communicate. Like the logical steps in accomplishing a task, these preparations can lead to an open, constructive relationship. In a partnership we need to agree on our plan. Whether we're working on a task or the relationship, we cannot proceed without a plan.

Step 2: Do

 We carry out our plan. We do the activity. We solve problems, make decisions, and communicate just as we planned we would.

Step 3: Check

 Did we follow our plan? Did we end up where we thought we would? Did the relationship work out as planned? The phrase "reality check" is popular in business discussions today. This is because we can get so wrapped up in activity, in the busyness of working hard, that we forget to stand back and see how we're doing. In this step, we should just observe how well we've implemented our plans. What new information do we need to consider in the partnership?

Step 4: Act

 Our reality check should either reinforce the efficacy of our process or help us understand just where our process has broken down. We can learn to improve our planning in the first step. We can recommit to executing our plan better in the second step. Perhaps we should evaluate more frequently in the third step. What can we improve on? How can we do better? We study the results of our process, draw conclusions, and decide how we will act right now. What's the best decision we can make in the moment?

Abandon

 Sometimes the action we should take is to simply abandon the activity. Suppose we discover that we do not play well together. This is the perfect time—*before* we have too much invested in the partnership—to acknowledge the fact, pick up our toys, and move on. Companies frequently find that their cultures or technologies are not as compatible as they thought. Rather than continuing down a path to nowhere, it's best sometimes to acknowledge the fact and look for a new partner. This is a healthy sign of maturity and growth. Like couples dating, you learn something about your partner. And just as important, you learn something about yourself. You have just increased your partnering intelligence.

Back to Step 1: Plan

 Because of what you've learned, you're now smarter and better able to incorporate this new learning into the next phase of the Plan–Do–Check–Act cycle. Now you reenter the cycle with a new plan, new knowledge, and increased potential for success. The cycle is a reminder that whether you're doing a task or developing a relationship, it's important to build quality into the process. The Plan–Do–Check–Act cycle provides a framework within which both task and relationship activities can develop.

Estimating how much time to spend in each stage can help teams plan timelines effectively. Successful teams split their time into three periods (see Figure 4). They spend about one-third of their time in the *planning* stage. (The time spent in the planning stage is split, with about one-third of the time spent on developing the task and two-thirds spent on the relationship components of the activity.) Groups spend about one-third of their time in the *doing* stage. (I encourage groups to spend about two-thirds of this time involved in tasks and about one-third of their time on relationship development.) Groups spend the final one-third of their time *checking* the activity and *acting* on the results. (This last period is generally split 50/50 between task and relationship activities.)

PAST VERSUS FUTURE ORIENTATION ENVIRONMENT

Over the years I've noticed that certain environments are lethal to partnerships. Like the human body, partnerships flourish in supportive atmospheres and die in toxic environments. I have labeled these environments "past and future orientations." Both orientations have specific characteristics and related behavior. They also tend to be endemic within the organization—that is, if you find them in one part of the organization, you'll usually find them throughout the organization. This is especially true if leadership embodies one or the other paradigm.

The concept of past versus future orientation is a paradox: it is intangible and yet very real. Organizations, like individuals, view their

Planning Stage	Doing Stage	Checking & Acting Stages
Task 33%	Task 67%	Task 50%
Relationship 67%	Relationship 33%	Relationship 50%

Figure 4   Timeline for a Successful Partnership

world through the "lens" formed by a set of strongly held beliefs. In a family, the parents hold this set of beliefs. In organizations, these beliefs are held by leadership. If I hold a certain view of something, then when I look though my lens, I'll see what I expect to see.

Let me give an example. Let's say that every time you invite me to dinner I'm a half-hour late. In time, you come to believe that I'll always be a half-hour late. You may compensate by making my invitation a half-hour earlier, based on my past behavior. This thinking reflects a past orientation. A future orientation might look something like this: You invite me to dinner. You say, "Steve, I'd really like to have you show up at 7:30 PM and not at 8:00 PM because it throws off my timing. Would you mind showing up on time?" Now you've switched your paradigm to a future perspective. If I agree, then you'll determine my trustworthiness based on my time of arrival. Rather than planning on my past behavior, we negotiated future behavior and will monitor it to see if I did what I said I would do. This is a future orientation.

Past/future orientation environment is endemic from a systems perspective. In other words, if I have a past orientation, I probably have certain characteristics that reinforce my perspective. To illustrate the systemic impact of past/future orientation, I have created Chart 1, Moving from a Past to a Future Orientation Environment. Note how it is necessary to address several attributes in order to make progress. When you practice win-win conflict resolution or increase your level of self-disclosure, for example, you move toward a future orientation. As you move toward the future orientation, trust begins to build in the partnership. And since establishing trust is a key skill, this in turn increases your partnering intelligence.

Chart 1

Moving from a Past to a Future Orientation Environment

To Move from a Past Orientation to a Future Orientation . . .	Increase Your Intelligence in This Attribute:
To move from "Relies on past history for decision making" to "Looks to the future with a clear vision" . . .	• Comfort with interdependence • Comfort with change • Ability to trust • Self-disclosure and feedback
To move from "Maintains status quo while resisting change" to "Welcomes change" . . .	• Comfort with change • Ability to trust • Win-win orientation • Self-disclosure and feedback
To move from "Desires to win conflicts" to "Creatively resolves conflicts" . . .	• Win-win orientation • Self-disclosure and feedback • Comfort with change • Ability to trust
To move from "Values independence" to "Values interdependence" . . .	• Self-disclosure and feedback • Win-win orientation • Ability to trust • Future orientation decision-making style
To move from "Has low trust of others" to "Creates trust through actions and words" . . .	• Comfort with change • Win-win orientation • Comfort with interdependence • Self-disclosure and feedback
To move from "Keeps information to self" to "Openly self-discloses information" . . .	• Comfort with change • Win-win orientation • Ability to trust • Self-disclosure and feedback • Comfort with interdependence • Future orientation decision-making style

STEP BY STEP

Now that you've had an overview of the Partnership Continuum model, are you ready to investigate each step and learn how to apply it? In each of the next four chapters, I'll address one of the stages of partnership development: assessing, exploring, initiating, and commiting. I focus on these stages because these are the tasks you'll engage in with your partners. And as you engage in the tasks, you'll automatically begin to move through the stages of relationship development. At each step along the way, I'll point out the tasks that need to happen to ensure that the partnership is balanced. And I'll identify the stage of relationship development you're in during each stage of partnership development.

For each stage of partnership development, I present two case studies. These real-world examples will describe for you how others have used the Partnership Continuum model and help you benchmark your progress against theirs.

CHAPTER FOUR

Assessing Stage

What Do You Want?

With the exception of the hermit on the top of the most isolated mountain in the world, there is virtually no one who has never formed a partnership. Even our hermit grew up somewhere with someone before trekking off to seek wisdom. For most of us, our family experience made an indelible mark on our ability to partner, whether good or bad. The ability to form good partnerships is closely linked with our ability to have good relationships. If we have poor relationships—if we find it stressful to make and keep good relationships—then partnering will be difficult for us. One of the keys to partnering is the ability to form good relationships. We need to be adept in the skills that allow us to get our needs met while helping others achieve their needs, too. Yet many of us do not have these skills—or if we do, we forget them when we're in situations that cause stress, fear, or anxiety. When we face these feelings, our instincts kick in. We turn to the innate fight or flight strategies to resolve our anguish. Whatever strategy we use to help us cope with our feelings, at some level we know that our "win" is only temporary and the next conflict is just around the corner.

What this does, to millions of us, is set up a pattern based on our mental maps. This pattern teaches us that relationships are bad, or difficult at best, and must be avoided at all costs. It doesn't take a Ph.D. to figure out the next step in this chain of logic: (relationships = pain) means (partnerships = pain).

ARE YOU READY?

So what happens when we can't fathom the concept of having a partnership? We begin to create a past orientation for ourselves—a series of reinforcing cause-and-effect events. First we refuse to trust relationships because of past experiences. We become afraid of getting hurt. Using old mental maps and remembering the times we were hurt, we end up trapping ourselves: When a new relationship occurs, it becomes a self-fulfilling prophecy reinforcing the hurt and pain. Consequently we choose to go it alone, which reinforces our desire to be independent. As change becomes more and more difficult, we spend more and more energy maintaining the status quo: a comfortable, safe place. We live in a past orientation because there is no trust. There is no trust because we are unwilling to open up to others by self-disclosing. The cycle continues to reinforce the belief. People sense this closedness and move away from us. People are attracted to openness; they shy away from those who are closed. Those who cannot trust choose a win-lose style of conflict resolution because they cannot trust anyone enough to collaborate. And so the cycle continues.

For the individual, life without partnerships is a lonely place. For a business, the inability to form partnerships will probably mean a slow and excruciating death in the marketplace as competitors become more adept at adapting to the new reality of interdependence in the twenty-first century.

To move from no partnership, the first thing you need to do is figure out what you want. To begin, fill out the Partnership Readiness Inventory (Exercise 1). This may give you some insight into how ready your organization is to form a partnership. The questions are designed to help you determine if a partnership is right for your organization.

BEGINNING THE ASSESSMENT

Now that you've decided you want a partnership, you are about to undertake perhaps the most difficult task of the partnering process: assessing your organization to determine its needs. This stage frequently requires the most time. Consistent with the Plan–Do–Check–Act cycle, the time is spent planning for what you want from the partnership and the quality of partnership you desire.

Exercise 1. Partnership Readiness Inventory

Question	Yes	No
Can you satisfy all your business requirements internally or by yourself?		
Are you satisfied with the way people are interacting within your organization?		
If other organizations in your industry have formed partnerships, have you?		
Is your culture receptive to partnering?		
Is your organizational culture based on a future orientation?		
Inside your organization, do individuals and departments work together to resolve problems?		
Do you believe organizational leadership wants to form a partnership?		

Interpreting the Results

If you answered no to three or more of these questions, you may want to reconsider your organization's readiness to form partnerships. Three or more no's to these questions demonstrate a tendency to be closed and to cling to a past orientation. Serious thought should be given to the organizational culture. Someone with influence in this situation should bring leadership together to discuss the implications of the organizational culture. Management must determine whether the organization is missing opportunities for growth and profit by being so closed. The discussion should investigate the desirability and potential benefits of creating partnerships with employees, departments, vendors, suppliers, or customers. If you answered yes to five or more of these questions, your organization is ready for the first stage of partnership development, assessing.

An internal assessment is a voyage of discovery, not an exercise in passing judgment. It's a chance to step back and, using a formal approach, take an objective look at the organization. It's an opportunity to update your mental maps and be objective about what you want. It can be a renewing exercise—reminding you that you're on the right track. It can also serve as a tool to discover gaps between where you think you are and what the assessment reveals. The realization may shake you up. Whether it confirms you're on the right track or it redirects your energies, you win because you're smarter. You've just increased your PQ.

Various occasions trigger assessments. The challenges inherent in new working arrangements, partnerships, mergers, or layoffs often necessitate self-examination. Changes in markets, personnel, and even sales patterns force companies to take a look at where they've been, where they are, and where they want to go.

Creating an Assessment Team

When I work with organizations to create a partnership, I have them assemble an assessment team. The role of this team is to:

- Determine the purpose of the assessment
- Define the scope of the assessment
- Bring a balanced perspective
- Embody varied skills and perspectives of the organization
- Act as the focal point of the effort
- Make decisions
- Communicate decisions
- Develop strategies, tactics, and timelines
- Create the implementation plan
- Identify and obtain resources

An internal assessment can be threatening. Senior managers have nearly begged me not to pursue an internal assessment. One vice president of quality told me she couldn't support a quality assessment in her business. She asked what other way I could get the information "I" needed without "upsetting" the employees. Her attitude was a red flag that more groundwork would need to be done before the assessment could be helpful to her. An internal assessment is threatening to people because their job performance will be examined and their ego is invested in past achievements. As manager of a department, you may feel that you've done a pretty good job. Now others are suddenly suggesting new directions, new requirements, and possibly other changes. And they are asking questions and poking around. Even though you think you've done a good job, you feel defensive. In an organization with a closed culture or a past orientation, protecting the status quo is the order of the day. You feel threatened by the assessment because you're not sold on the idea of change—and it's change that is prompting the assessment.

The assessment must be a voluntary activity. Unless the owners of the assessment want the information, good or bad, they'll discount the results. They may ignore any information that's hard for them to accept. When people are threatened by an assessment, they'll quibble about the methodology, the timing, or the questions. Discrediting the assessment is a common tactic used by management in past-orientation organizations. They can't bear the thought of shaking up the status quo, so they shoot the message and usually the messenger, too. Without leadership's support from the outset, an assessment is likely to fail in such organizations.

The patient who refuses to have checkups runs the risk of minor problems becoming unmanageable. The driver who ignores the auto mechanic's dire diagnosis does so at the risk of breaking down later in heavy traffic. So, too, do organizations that refuse to conduct internal assessments.

Approaching an Internal Assessment

I approach the internal assessment from a simple perspective: "What can I learn?" and "What's in it for me?" The purpose of conducting an internal assessment is to help people or organizations focus on the aspects of a partnership that will help them attain their goals. The assessment looks at the past and present in order to understand the strengths, weaknesses, assets, and needs of the organization. The internal assessment presents the organization with a systematic approach to collecting information from many sources.

Inclusion is a guideline that can never steer you wrong. Anyone who might be affected should join in the assessment process, and those most affected should participate from the beginning. It is perhaps more effective to determine who should be left out of this process. If you can't justify leaving people out, invite them in. Not only do people need to present their own wish lists, but they may well be sources of potential partners for the organization.

Not including someone may lead to serious consequences later. A person who's left out may think the worst: "Are they trying to eliminate me? What's this all about? Why am I not being included?" When I worked as an internal consultant on the organizational effectiveness team with a telephone company, the company's leaders didn't like the information we reported. In fact, the president contracted with an outside consulting group to come in and assess our internal consulting group. This outside firm found conducting the assessment a frustrating experience—so frustrating that they cited the company as one of the most difficult clients they'd ever encountered. They went so far as to report that their efforts were "sabotaged" and the reliability of their assessment was compromised due to lack of cooperation. Ultimately they advised against basing any future decisions on their internal assessment. They felt it was a waste of their time and the company's money. Leadership's mistake was pitting one group against another instead of having the two teams work together. Had the president encouraged the latter strategy, the internal consultants could have advised the outside consultants about company culture and the political landscape. At the same time, the outside consultants could have contributed a fresh and objective perspective.

While inclusion is important, it may not be practical or even wise to involve everyone in the internal assessment from the start. One strategy I use is to involve different groups at different stages. You may start with key leadership and then, once you have their commitment, begin to move down the organization. As you assess various areas of the organization, you begin to involve those people in the assessment. As you do, be sure to communicate clearly the purpose and scope of the assessment to alleviate fears.

While you may not be able to involve everyone, it's essential to communicate information about the assessment to people inside the organization. Tell them what you know, what you are doing, and why. Be as honest and open as you can. It's a great first step in moving along the Partnership Continuum and increasing your partnering intelligence.

ASSESSING THE ETHEREAL
AND MATERIAL ORGANIZATION

Once the organization has decided to conduct an internal assessment, leadership must decide what it wants the assessment to focus on. Most organizations look at only one area of the organization: the tasks. Some

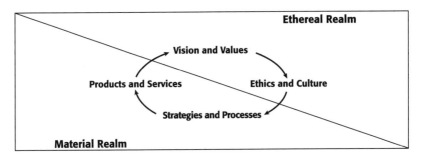

Figure 5 Holistic Organization Model

organizations may assess employee morale through the use of an employee survey—an example of examining the atmosphere of the organization. But in forming a partnership, both of these areas need attention. I call them the ethereal and material realms of the organization (see Figure 5). I use the word *realm* because it describes the degree to which these spheres interact while still maintaining separate energies and characteristics. Let me use an analogy to show how these realms relate to partnerships. On planet Earth, there are two primary realms of existence. One is the marine habitat and the other is terrestrial. While each of these realms operates independently of the other, the two interact in significant ways. For example, they create the weather systems that influence all life in both realms. The maritime environ affects the atmosphere by heating or cooling more slowly than the surrounding landmasses and providing the moisture that evaporates into the air. In a series of geoclimatic steps, weather is then circulated around the globe in a series of patterns that support the life forms that have developed in these environments. It is a system. Organizations operate in atmospheres, too. And since organizations are systems, too, the atmosphere affects all aspects of the organization.

Traditional approaches to organizational improvement tend to focus on the material realm of the business. They seek to manage the strategies, processes, products, and services we believe will most influence the bottom line. Recently the U.S. Postal Service overhauled its strategies and processes to defend itself in the competitive marketplace. But little attention was paid to the relationships between managers and employees. Managers, employees, and their unions acted as if their business was invulnerable. They were wrong. It is the *spirit* of the business that will ultimately determine its success in the marketplace. How did you feel the last time you were in a post office and an indifferent clerk ignored you? This is not to say a business can have bad strategies and processes delivering unwanted goods and services. Rather, the goods and services will reflect on the organization's ethereal energies—that is, its vision, values, and ethics, and the culture that results.

If you don't understand these unseen aspects of the business, you may not understand why the visible portions are not working very well. When forming a partnership, it's important to understand all the influences on the business—including the unseen portions. In my experience, it's the unseen portions that have the greatest impact on an organization's success.

The Ethereal Realm: Vision, Values, Ethics, and Culture

In the conceptual stage, top leadership envisions the purpose, scope, and potential outcomes of the internal assessment. Conceptual development must include the interests of those for whom the partnership is being created. The conceptual stage of the internal assessment is a spiritual look at the organization. This requires the people involved to look at the organization's heart and soul as well as its related material outputs: strategies and processes.

By understanding the heart and soul of the organization, we become grounded with our internal security, and have a foundation for our ethical standards. These ethereal qualities are what enable us to harness the organization's energy to accomplish tasks. It is the ethereal energies of the organization that connect everyone's energy like an electronic grid. This energy motivates, focuses, and moves people in one direction or another. Have you ever walked into an office and felt the tension? The ethereal plane manifests itself through the *morale* of the organization. When morale is high, people show high productivity and creativity and solve problems easily. When morale is low, people struggle.

Like the human spirit, ethereal energy exists. Whether or not we are conscious of its influence, it is real and shapes what we do. We recognize a feeling of unity and common purpose. Have you ever seen people rally energy—as when a sports team is winning? We've all experienced occasions when team spirit seemed to propel the whole group toward extraordinary performance. On the other hand, maybe you can remember times when your group had low morale and couldn't perform or lacked the energy to achieve anything noteworthy.

This is an important concept to keep in mind when creating partnerships. For the Partnership Continuum to work, you need to balance the energy in the alliance between the two aspects of partnering: tasks and relationships. If you don't understand the relationship aspects of the organization, you won't be able to find the necessary balance in partnering.

Recently I participated in a strategic planning session for a large credit card company. Management was composed of intelligent people who were very competitive. I witnessed the group mire itself in a pointless discussion about whether to use the word *understand* or the word *validate* in a statement about client relationships. For two hours the group looped back to this discussion again and again. But the issue blocking the group's progress wasn't about words at all—a dictionary had clarified their meanings early on. Instead, two powerful individuals vying for control drove the dynamics of the group's experience. Even at the expense of the group's time and the outcome of the process, they needed to satisfy their egos.

Forcing your ego on others and striving to control people and events are negative ethereal energies that discourage teamwork and produce resentment. Ego needs have crumbled empires; they can certainly derail a company's strategic plan. In partnerships, ego-driven discussions sap people's energy and disillusion them from accomplishing tasks.

As shown in Figure 5, ethereal energies (the vision, values, ethics, and culture of the organization) determine the quality of its strategies and processes, and ultimately of its products and services. The value and the potential of the organization's business are defined by ethereal energies and manifest themselves in the strategies and processes they produce.

An organization's ethereal energies are evident to the consumers who purchase products and services. Recently an automaker recalled a pickup truck. The recall was to insert a small, inexpensive part that management felt was unnecessary and had elected to leave out of the production process. This part prevented gasoline from slipping back onto a hot manifold and possibly causing a fire. Leaving the part out saved the manufacturer pennies per vehicle.

After a series of fires, however, this manufacturer was taken to court. Costly court expenses and victim settlements eventually forced the manufacturer to install this device. Had the company placed profits over people? Ever since I learned of this case, I haven't considered buying one of that company's vehicles. Knowing its values, how could I ever trust it for my safety? In the short run, the bottom-line decision looked good. In the long run, however, the decision reduced the bottom-line profits and cost the company potential business as well.

Our attitudes—and consequently our behavior toward others—are influenced by our fundamental psychological mind-set toward abundance (or scarcity). If we believe that the market is wide open, for instance, we'll be more likely to share what we have in order to build on it. This represents a future orientation. But if we believe the market is shrinking, that our share of that market is threatened, we'll probably dig in to protect what we have. Believing resources are scarce, we'll behave more defensively, in a past-orientation mind-set. What determines our outlook, for either abundance or scarcity, has more to do with our attitude than with reality. The opportunities for companies to prosper by creating better internal and external partnerships are limited only by their own attitudes toward the future. Companies increase their PQ by adopting an attitude of abundance. This is because they move from a past orientation to a future orientation by looking for possibilities—thereby generating creativity and mutual benefits.

Organizations with no mission beyond the pursuit of money, power, or material well-being are shortsighted. These are legitimate goals, but they're not visionary. They don't relate to the concept of abundance because they're too narrow. In short, they don't satisfy ethereal needs. These are the basic human needs to belong, to contribute, to share, and to be valued as part of a system. An enterprise that inspires people has to represent more than just the pursuit of profits—especially if everyone doesn't share in the profits. Partnering is one strategy to connect the ethereal needs of people in the workplace with the tasks of the business. Although more organizations are spreading equity stakes around to more people, often the profits end up with shareholders or are plowed back into the company's assets. This is not to say that employees can't invest in the company in other ways. It's just that too often companies assume that what the owners want will satisfy workers as well. Often it doesn't. And there goes the balance between task and relationship.

Organizations, like teams, operate best when everyone contributes to the organizational goals. When parts merely work together collectively, they focus only on their own domain—on their own success or survival. We might work hard to attain the output expected by others, but only in ways that ensure our individual success. When we look at ourselves as a system, however, we begin to integrate our functions and modify them to support others. Imagine an orchestra showing up to play with no program, no sheet music, and no conductor. No one communicates a vision of the musical outcome. Forty musicians, all virtuosos in their own right, would produce something short of the orchestra's potential without the organization inspired by the conductor's vision. Now imagine this same group of musicians guided by the leader, all on the same page of music, all blending their individual performances to produce an outcome. The audience is moved; emotions are stirred; the box office is happy.

Vision and Values

Creating and articulating vision and values is a basic leadership role. Some people mistrust the concept of vision and values in organizations. Organizational leaders don't want to waste time creating yet another useless description of the future, and employees grow weary of hearing lofty ideals mouthed by their leaders. Phony visions do nothing but reinforce their cynicism. In an organization with a past orientation, actions speak louder than words. People watch what others do, not what they say. Organizations must act in accordance with their vision every day—instead of treating the concept as a training exercise that they'll update every five years.

A vision is not a goal. It's not a statement that points toward a destination. Margaret J. Wheatley (1992) expresses this concept eloquently in her book *Leadership and the New Science*. She explains how a vision is really a field of energy:

Vision—the need for organizational clarity about purpose and direction—is a wonderful candidate for field theory. In linear fashion, we have most often conceived of vision as thinking into the future, creating a *destination* for the organization. We have believed that the clearer the image of the destination, the more force the future will exert on the present, pulling us into that desired future state. It's a very strong Newtonian image, much like the old view of gravity. But what if we changed the science and looked at vision as a field? What if we saw a field of vision that needed to permeate organizational space, rather than viewing vision as a linear destination? (pp. 53–54)

Permeating the organization means that the vision itself becomes an energy form that influences the human energies that run the business. Statements that only talk about achieving a goal or arriving at a linear point in the future don't have the power that Wheatley describes. I know of a telecommunications company whose vision statement reads: "By the year 2000, we will be the finest company in the world connecting people with their world." This statement uses a point on a timeline as a destination. The statement is closed and limited. Once the calendar reads 2000, what happens? It's an extrinsic statement that focuses achievement on something external to themselves.

An open, intrinsic vision statement would read something like one international investment firm's: "We are committed to building positive futures, one relationship at a time." This company understands the value of the ethereal energy inherent in the process of doing business. It acknowledges that good things will result from the way we do business, not just what may appear on a future balance statement.

Ethics and Culture

Discussing ethics is awkward because people feel so strongly about them. Ethics aren't universally shared or even understood, and their application in practice is always an issue. Our difficulty in talking about ethical situations may be due to the fact that no one wants to be labeled "unethical." Yet every organization should ask itself daily: "Are we an ethical organization?" The question is pretty provocative.

Ethics are based on individual behavior. Organizations do not have ethics; the people in the organization have ethics. Leaders show others their ethical standards by what they do, and the other people in the organization most likely rise or sink to their standards. Everyone in the company is affected when a leader makes a policy decision or

Exercise 2. Culture Questionnaire	
Question	**Attribute**
1. How much do you trust the leadership?	• Ability to trust
2. Do you feel included in organizational decisions?	• Past/future orientation in decision making
3. Are information and data shared with you?	• Self-disclosure and feedback
4. Do you feel management listens to you?	• Past/future orientation in decision making • Self-disclosure and feedback
5. How open do you feel the organization is with you?	• Past/future orientation in decision making • Ability to trust • Self-disclosure and feedback
6. How are conflicts resolved in this organization?	• Win-win orientation
7. Does this organization take risks?	• Ability to trust • Past/future orientation in decision making
8. How does this organization respond to change?	• Comfort with change • Ability to trust

when an owner decides to commit a company to a certain course. In other words, everyone is affected by the leaders' ethical standards. Looking at your company's vision is a way to reflect on its ethical standards. Revising, expanding, or changing the company's vision is a way for the assessment step to launch the partnership. We also need to examine the culture of our organization.

A questionnaire can provide remarkable insight into the culture. And the people who live in the culture are the best ones to supply the data. When discussing partnerships, I ask the leadership to respond to a questionnaire about the organization's culture (see Exercise 2). The matrix shows how each aspect of the organization's culture relates to the six attributes on the Partnership Continuum.

Exercise 3. Past/Future Orientation Environment

The following graph often helps people talk about how they view the company. One end of the graph is labeled *past* and the other end *future*. Based on the characteristics of past and future orientation from the Partnership Continuum, mark the place where you see your organization on this continuum.

Past   **Future**

Exercise 3 offers a simple line graph format for assessing an organization's past or future orientation environment. The information mined from this simple exercise is very important. Above all, it gives a quick self-assessment of where people see the organization.

People from departments, branches, or any other unit can combine their estimates and analyze their group rating. Some departments may identify themselves as being close to the future orientation end of the spectrum; others may see themselves at the opposite end. As shown in Figure 6, graphing each department should help identify prospective areas where readiness for partnering activities is evident—and indicate where more developmental activities are needed before the decision to create a partnership is made.

By doing Exercises 2 and 3, you are starting to gather information about where the organization sees itself in terms of past and future orientation. Remember that you are just starting the journey of partnering. Most organizations that are just starting to form partnerships have past orientation environments.

Articulating a vision that is consistent with the leadership's actions and cultural readiness can motivate everyone to participate in its implementation. Goals such as sales targets, revenue growth, and market penetration are strategic directions that organizations should address in their mission statements. But without a vision to channel the ethereal energies of each participant, such goals alone are not compelling enough to break through to the creative zone.

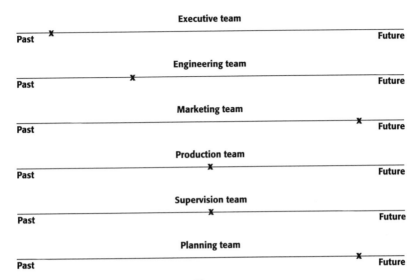

Figure 6 Past/Future Orientation Profile

The Material Realm: Strategies, Processes, Products, and Services

Frederick W. Taylor was an American engineer and efficiency expert who experimented in improving production in the early 1900s. He sought, as many businesses still do, to dissect work in organizations in a quest to use scientific, quantitative measurement to improve processes. Time-study engineers tried to make these processes more efficient. By simplifying the work, they planned to reduce labor costs. They presumed because the task was simpler, they could use cheaper, less educated, less skilled workers.

What resulted in many organizations was a workforce that functioned not as integrated units benefiting the whole but as separate units focused on their own existence. The engineers ignored what they couldn't measure. They could measure material output. They could measure product quality, levels of service, production and sales activity, and even profit. What they couldn't measure were the ethereal qualities of the enterprise: the vision, values, ethics, and culture. They focused on the material realm and ignored the ethereal realm since it couldn't be measured. In this case, engineering didn't guarantee anything but successful engineering.

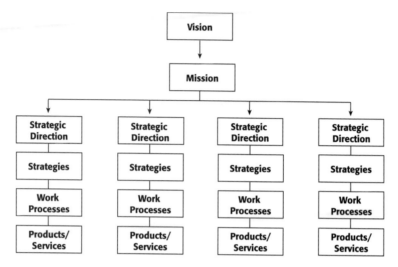

Figure 7 Organizational Process Model

What Frederick W. Taylor did, in effect, was cut workers off from the ethereal qualities of their work by focusing their contribution on the task. This explains why assembly-line workers frequently describe their work as mindless and soulless. Organizations in the new economy are going to have to unlearn some of Taylor's lessons since the new economy will have little to do with putting widgets together. Technology is making repetitive manual labor obsolete by automating much of it with robotics. To accomplish the organization's vision, employees operating in the new economy will need a holistic understanding of the business in partnership with other stakeholders.

To assess the gap between where the organization wants to be and what it currently can produce, I use the organizational process model (Figure 7). This tool helps me view the organization at the macro level. The purpose in completing an organizational process model is to show, at a single glance, what the organization is accomplishing from a task perspective. It indicates visually whether the work being done is consistent with the organization's vision and mission. Moreover, the model identifies any gaps between present processes and future plans.

A credit card company I worked with had its genesis in the postwar boom of the 1950s and 1960s, enabling millions of consumers to buy electrical appliances. Although this company had been very successful for decades, competition for market share of appliances increased as the market became saturated. In addition, the spread of other credit resources began to squeeze this company's profits. Soon the company was expanding into other kinds of businesses including dealer financing, retail space design, inventory financing, and even financing capital improvements for dealers. Each area now competed for the resources of the original credit card business, and the company found itself spread too thin. Divisions competed against each other for personnel and budget. And as the top leadership increasingly abandoned initiatives that didn't produce short-term profits, the whole company's morale spiraled downward. The demise of this company is probably due not to any single factor or even to poor business decisions, but to a lack of focus on vision. At the very least its vision became blurred. Scrambling with temporary solutions failed to address this company's fundamental issue. As its market changed, it needed to clarify and expand its vision rather than busy itself with diversions.

As the vision defines the ethereal qualities of the organization, the mission statement defines the task functions. It states how the vision will be accomplished. Generally the *mission statement* defines the area of the organization's expertise and targets a specific industry or population. The Minnesota Council for Preventive Medicine, a nonprofit organization of physicians, has a mission statement that reads:

> To promote preventive medicine in Minnesota, our goals include:
>
> • To create a network of physicians interested in preventive medicine
>
> • To offer expertise in preventive medicine to interested individuals, organizations, learning institutions, and media
>
> • To influence public policy toward the prevention of physical and mental illness and injury
>
> • To support and promote specific initiatives that seek to prevent illness and injury

This mission statement clearly defines the areas this council intends to influence and the methods it will use. It defines how the organization will achieve its vision.

The *strategic directions* are the broad areas in which the organization will focus its energy. Organizations frequently use pluralistic approaches to achieve success. A company focuses its strategic directions by identifying the various market segments it serves, the groups of consumers it targets, or the industries in which it plans to compete. A sandwich company identified three market segments it wished to serve:

- Dine-in customers
- Take-out customers
- Delivery customers

After identifying its market segments, it put into place specific strategies and processes to serve each of these consumer groups.

Perhaps in the future the sandwich company could offer prepared sandwiches for sale in a grocery store as a fourth growth opportunity. This could present a chance to develop a partnership with a grocery store chain. Does this fit into its current strategic directions? At the moment it does not, since the three strategic directions it has identified are focused on other delivery systems. Nevertheless, it could expand its strategic directions to include grocery store customers and significantly increase its potential market. By taking an inventory of strategic directions, an organization can determine what partnerships are appropriate today and look toward expanding its business in the future.

Strategies detail what you are going to do to get where you've said you want to go. In the example of the sandwich chain, the organization planned to install drive-through windows at all its restaurants to meet the needs of its take-out customers. Strategies relate to meeting customer needs and are implemented by processes developed to carry out the strategy.

Work processes are how the strategies will be implemented. They are the actions that fulfill the strategy and meet the specific needs of the customer. The most successful organizations use process management—a business science that documents, measures, analyzes, and improves its processes. The sandwich chain, for instance, has an order-taking process, a sandwich-making process, a dining-room–cleaning process, a supply-ordering process, and many other processes that support its strategies of serving its customers. By using structured methodologies such as process management, an organization controls the quality and reliability of its product or service to enhance its success in the marketplace.

By now you may be wondering what all this has to do with partnerships. Having the ability to map out your vision, mission statement, strategic directions, and processes will enable you to figure out the direction you want to move. Understanding your business from this holistic perspective gives a total picture of what's happening now. Upon reflection, you can start to assemble the pieces for the next future state. Understanding your business and its processes is a key to determining your needs. Once these needs have been identified, you've increased your partnering intelligence. Now you're in a better position to start the exploring stage described in Chapter 5.

IDENTIFYING NEEDS

The self-assessment process gives us an updated view of who we are. Organizations that commit to this process know their leadership style, express their visions for the future, and devise strategies and processes to realize that future. Here's where a critical question emerges: To get where we want to go, can we use the resources we already have? Or do we need to look for a partner?

At this point the organization has to think hard. The decision to go it alone—to forgo the partnership strategy and maximize or expand present resources through other means—may be the wisest alternative. The whole point of the assessing stage has been to secure a firm foundation for future growth. In the process, by using the Partnership Continuum as a guide, we can choose to move toward developing a partnership. Or, just as important, we can decide this is not our best route to the future. The internal assessment is needed to reveal our own interests and what we require in a partnership.

Cultural forces influence how well partnerships develop. Each company's management style, whether autocratic or consensus based, may be a factor. Is the organization's culture past oriented or future oriented? Is the corporate culture fear based or open? Are organizational structures flexible or rigid? Are partners willing to collaborate on all critical issues? In the exploring stage, as we shall see, we use this information to select, approach, and create an appropriate partner. But before taking this step, work through Exercises 4 and 5. By completing these exercises, you'll be in a good position to analyze your current situation. You have just increased your partnering intelligence. Now you can decide whether partnering is right for you—and if so, what characteristics you will be looking for in a future partner.

Exercise 4. Summary of the Assessing Stage

Question	Yes	No	Outcome/Comments
1. Have we committed our resources to a comprehensive assessment?			
2. Have we included all stakeholders?			
3. Have we identified ethereal qualities?			
4. Have we agreed on a company vision?			
5. Do we have a mission statement?			
6. Do we have written strategic goals?			
7. Do we know which processes we can use to achieve our goals?			
8. Is there a gap between where we are and where we want to be?			
9. What needs do we expect a partnership to satisfy?			
10. Are we ready, willing, and able to be a good partner?			

Exercise 5. Needs Assessment Tool

Step	Issue	Outcome	Recommendation
1. Contract with Participants • Identify team leadership • Leadership's expectations of assessment • Focus for assessment: task/relationship/both • Roles and responsibilities • Budget			
2. Research • Methodology (surveys, interviews, focus groups, questionnaires) • Research objectives • Scope of assessment • Time			

Exercise 5. Needs Assessment Tool *continued*			
Step	**Issue**	**Outcome**	**Recommendation**
3. Data Analysis • Types of data: qualitative/quantitative • Content analysis • Categories			
4. Presentation • Provide leadership with data • Gain leadership's validation of data • Get feedback on data			

5. Interpretation
• Ask leadership what data
  mean to them
• Provide insights into
  meaning of data
• Gain leadership's agreement
  on data interpretation			

6. Plan for Action
• Gain leadership's
  commitment to move ahead
• Prioritize critical areas
  for action
• Develop action plans for
  areas with high priority
• Identify organizational impact
• Focus on material/ethereal
• Continue to use PDCA cycle			

ASSESSING STAGE PLAN–DO–CHECK–ACT CYCLE

I have reviewed with you the importance of exploring both the ethereal and material realms of the organization. I have demonstrated the systemic nature of organizations and how vision, values, ethics, and culture affect the organizational mission, strategies, processes, products, and services. We have reviewed the steps and tools for conducting an internal needs assessment. Now it is time to build quality into the process by adhering to the Plan-Do-Check-Act cycle of continuous improvement. This is accomplished by listing the tasks that need to occur in the Assessing Stage under each step of the cycle. Below, I have put together a sample of what to do in each step. You may want to use this example as is or modify it to meet your particular objectives. Either way, it will help you accomplish the task in less time and with greater efficiency and higher quality.

PLAN

You have determined you are going to conduct the internal assessment.
- Select the assessment team.
- Review the ethereal areas of the organization (vision, values, ethics, culture).
- Review the material areas of the organization (strategies, processes, products, services).
- Identify the purpose, scope, and potential outcomes of the assessment.

DO

- Complete the Culture Questionnaire (Exercise 2).
- Develop a Past/Future Orientation Profile (Figure 6).
- Complete the Organizational Process Model (Figure 7).
- Complete the Needs Assessment Tool (Exercise 5).
- Using the assessment team, determine the areas that must be addressed For example, if you find you have ethereal issues that are preventing the organization from accomplishing its goals, list them. If there is a material area the organization is lacking, identify what it is you want to accomplish. Try using a matrix approach like the one shown in Chart 2.
- Assessment team completes Summary of the Assessing Stage (Exercise 4).

CHECK

- Did you attain your goals and objectives?
- If not, what did you forget?
- Review the output with your organization's leadership.
- Get leadership's response to the areas you cite as organizational needs.
- Are these needs consistent with the tribal wisdom of the organization?
- What surprises are there?
- What did you expect?

• What areas of the Summary of the Assessing Stage (Exercise 4) are missing?

• Do you need to revisit any of these areas for more information?

• Did you address the ethereal and material dimensions of the organization?

• Do you have plans to bring both dimensions into alignment with the Partnership Continuum?

ACT

At this point you need to go back to the assessing stage and readdress any areas that have not been covered adequately. If you think you have covered the areas to your assessment team's satisfaction and have pinpointed the needs of the organization, both ethereal and material, then you're ready to move on to the next stage of the Partnership Continuum: exploring.

Chart 2

Outcomes of the Needs Assessment Matrix (Sample Assessment)

Issue	Outcome	Recommendation
Past orientation environment	Lack of open communication between management and employees	Establish open communication between all levels in organization
	Lack of trust	Build trust by revealing plans and getting consensus
	Top-down decision making	Build team decision-making structure
Poor communication between Production and Marketing	Marketing and Production do not meet for planning	Marketing and Production develop joint strategy for sales initiatives
Off-site telemarketing sales of new Omega product line	Lack of sales capacity to market Omega product nationally	Partner with telemarketing firm to sell Omega nationally

PARTNERSHIP CASE STUDIES

I've worked with hundreds of organizations to help them form partnerships—both internally and with other organizations. The case studies I offer here are true and reflect normal behavior and the common reactions I get from the people I work with. These partnerships were successful, but not perfect. And that is the authentic value of the case studies. We see real people in real situations acting and reacting the way we ourselves might. Several questions are worth thinking about while following the case studies:

- What can I learn from this case study?
- What did these people do to increase their partnering intelligence?
- What could they have done to improve their partnership?

INTERNAL PARTNERSHIP: CONVENTION HOTEL

Marty and Jean were employees at a large convention hotel in Minneapolis. Marty was the supervisor of maintenance and Jean headed the housekeeping division. This 800-room hotel is part of an international chain of hotels. Marty had about forty house engineers on his staff and they were responsible for all building maintenance. Their duties varied from changing lightbulbs to fixing the hotel's heating and cooling systems. Jean managed a staff of about 100 housekeepers, groomers, and laundry personnel. Marty and Jean were constantly at each other's throats because of conflicts between the two departments. More than once they'd had separate meetings with Eric, the hotel's general manager, complaining about the other. It seems that housekeeping was constantly complaining that because maintenance would not clean up after themselves once they finished repairing something in a room, housekeeping had to redo the room. While this dispute may sound minor, it was the source of years of anger between these two employees. To make matters worse, Jean and Marty did not like each other personally. Jean told me she thought Marty was a bigot and a bully. Marty complained that Jean was overly sensitive and that her staff was lazy and whined constantly.

The general manager invited me in to help form a partnership between the two departments. I'll take you through the stages of development as we go through this and the next three chapters so you can witness firsthand how to use the Partnership Continuum to increase your PQ. I'll use the Plan–Do–Check–Act cycle to demonstrate how to weave the concept of continuous improvement into the process of developing a successful partnership.

The hotel general manager invited Marty and Jean to a meeting at which I was present. He suggested there had been a great deal of tension between the housekeeping staff and engineering. He wanted to know if the two departments couldn't somehow start to work together and form a partnership to better serve the guests and each other. Marty was immediately dubious. He didn't want to partner with Jean over anything. He said his group was doing just fine and from what he could tell, housekeeping was doing a good job, too. Jean said guests often complained that housekeeping had done a poor job of cleaning the room. She noticed that these were the rooms that had been scheduled for maintenance, and she was constantly sending housekeepers back to rooms where maintenance had just completed a job. She complained that the maintenance engineers made a mess and never cleaned up after themselves. Marty just smirked.

I suggested that we meet individually and talk about the problem. I first met with Marty. I wanted to know several things about Marty's operation. What was his vision of the maintenance organization in the hotel? He told me he wanted to make sure everything in each room operated properly and was in good repair. "But, you know, with 800 guest rooms, three dining rooms, fifteen meeting rooms, two kitchens, a laundry, and a suite of executive offices, it's impossible not to have something broken." I told him I could understand his point. When I asked about his relationship with Jean, he said she was all right "personally" but was overly sensitive to criticism and her staff was not always competent and frequently did a poor job and then blamed it on maintenance. Once I understood the relationship issues, I began to ask about the tasks. I asked how people got assigned jobs, the hours when people were scheduled, and other issues where I thought there might be conflicts. I got an understanding of how they measured their work and noted the performance issues that were important to them. Marty showed me a priority list of items that the maintenance people followed to help them get the job done.

Then I went to Jean and asked the same questions. Her vision was to have each guest be totally pleased with the cleanliness of the room and to have the room in perfect shape when guests arrived. I asked how she felt about maintenance. She said that Marty really didn't care about her or housekeeping: they were there to fix things and she was there to clean up after them. "That really annoys me," she said, "because we are not here to clean up after maintenance. We're here to ensure the comfort of our guests and make sure their rooms are cleaned. The engineers are supposed to clean up after themselves—and they've been told that a hundred times. They just don't care. And they know if they leave a mess it reflects on housekeeping, not them." I then asked her about the scheduling of the rooms for cleaning and the housekeepers. She provided me with all the details of the tasks.

After my discussions with Marty and Jean, I began to understand that they really had more in common than they thought. So I invited them both back to a meeting. At the meeting I showed them the Partnership Continuum and asked if they were interested in working through the model together. They both agreed. So I asked each of them to share their personal vision with the other. After they did so, I asked them to come up with a vision they could both agree on. Since they had so much in common, it was easy for them to do. The shared vision they agreed on was this: Each guest would have a clean room in which everything worked properly. After we all agreed on the vision, I asked about the two dynamics of the Partnership Continuum. First, I said, let's talk about the stages of relationship development. Both agreed they hadn't really gotten along in the past. In reality, they didn't even know each other very well. I asked them if they met frequently to discuss issues of mutual concern. I wasn't surprised to hear that they rarely even talked to each other, much less met. So I asked them what they could do to improve their relationship. Marty surprised me: "I think it would be helpful if we got to know each other's operations. Maybe there's some way we can work together to solve our issues." Jean immediately responded by suggesting they meet one afternoon the next week to talk about how each of them accomplishes his or her tasks.

The following week we met and both Jean and Marty reviewed how they scheduled and accomplished their tasks. One of the first things Jean noticed was that there was no coordination between cleaning the rooms and maintenance work. She asked Marty what time he received his list of guest room maintenance jobs. "First thing in the morning, about 7:30," he said. The job orders were collected by the chief operator and given to him. He then passed them out to the maintenance engineers. We were well on our way to identifying the needs.

EXTERNAL PARTNERSHIP: DOWNTOWN OFFICE TOWER

The city is in the midst of a building boom. All over downtown, the landscape is changing as office space gets tighter and towers sprout up on once-empty street-level parking lots. One of the city's largest, most prestigious contractors has just completed negotiations with a legal firm to build a new office tower. The location was selected and preliminary architectural design work completed. With the tight budget and time constraints, how could Robert, the contractor, get the job completed on time and on budget? The client was currently leasing fifteen stories and their lease was up at the end of the next year. They needed to have their new building finished by then.

Once the deal was signed, Robert went to work scoping out the project plan and timeline. Although he had completed many projects in the past, this one was special. The magnitude of the project, the prestigious location, and the building put additional pressure on him to make sure the project went off without a hitch. Constructing a thirty-seven-story building is a complex task. Coordinating the numerous variables can strain the best project manager's partnering intelligence. But nothing is quite so critical, or as potentially stressful, as the labor issue. Not only is labor one of the biggest expenses, it could be the one most easily mismanaged. Robert remembered one project when an electrical union had walked off the job. Not only did the strike shut down the entire project for over a month, but once it was settled, it took three weeks just to reorganize the project timeline—not to mention the headache caused by all the building materials arriving with no place to store them. It cost everyone a bundle in lost time, money, and goodwill.

Robert called Peter at the city's Building and Construction Trades Council. Peter is responsible for negotiating partnerships between the local union building trades and building contractors. Having worked with Peter in the past, Robert knew that he and Peter could figure out a way to meet each other's needs. Robert set up a meeting. In most cases, an organization would conduct a needs assessment to figure out what they needed in a partnership. But in this case, both Robert and Peter knew exactly what they needed from each other. They had partnered before on many successful projects. Robert's primary concern was to have the building completed on time. Second to this he needed to meet the tight budgetary guidelines given to him by the client. Naturally the budget proposal sent out requests for pricing to many different subcontractors. Since pricing was a concern, he knew he needed something more from Peter than just a time commitment. He needed to be sure the bids were competitive. He wanted to use union labor, but the price had to be right.

At the meeting, Robert began to express his needs. If he and the unions were to be partners, he needed a no-strike agreement and a commitment to provide the skilled and licensed labor when required—and the bids needed to be competitive with nonunion labor. Peter's top priority was simple: The workplace had to be a union work site with all-union labor. He also wanted to be sure that negotiated wages and benefits were paid to the trade members and that management followed union work and safety rules. Based on their discussion, both determined that they could satisfy each other's needs. They agreed to explore what it would take to partner on this project.

CHAPTER FIVE

Exploring Stage
Meeting the Right Partner

You've assessed your ability to meet your own needs and have noted a gap between your future goals and present capabilities. You've looked at your organization and concluded that partnering with another could help you fill this gap. You've judged your capacity to be a good partner by understanding the ethereal and material realms of your organization. You've gathered information about your needs and wants. You're ready, willing, and able to be a good partner. You are now in the exploring stage.

When Northwest Airlines completed its internal assessment, it discovered that it was the strongest competitor from the North American market across the Pacific to the Asian markets. But it also discovered that its flights across the North Atlantic into the European market were far from dominant. It had some flights to Frankfurt and London, but the competition across the Atlantic was stiff. The airline also recognized that its fleet of aircraft was not large enough to compete in the number of cities the European market offered. Northwest's leadership believed they could be a good partner for someone else in that they had a clear mission and a lot of new, enthusiastic people running the company. Relations between management and unions were improving.

Northwest decided to try a "hub and spoke" strategy that had worked well in the North American market. The hub and spoke concept means that airplanes fly to a central location and then fan out to distant points. After comparing profiles of several European airlines, Northwest selected KLM of the Netherlands as a good candidate for its needs. It also saw how it could help KLM expand in two areas: the North American and Asian markets. KLM had an extensive route structure in Europe and a large, modern facility at Schipol Airport in Amsterdam, which is centrally located. On paper at least, the partnership between these two carriers appeared ideal.

WHAT TYPE OF PARTNERSHIP DO YOU WANT?

Some partnerships are obvious right from the start. Suppose a company wants to partner with its employees' union to start a quality improvement process. Or perhaps a company wants to have two or more departments such as manufacturing, marketing, or engineering partner on a product development project. Or a natural alliance between a customer and supplier results from the relationship already in place.

A less obvious partnership would be in the development of new products, services, or technologies designed to meet future customer needs. New partnerships offer the opportunity to be partners by design. These new partnerships offer more options because the organization is limited only by its imagination. But selecting the right partner can be a daunting experience if key decisions about the purpose of the partnership are not clear from the beginning.

A systematic approach to finding a partner works best. Generally my clients have some concept of who they might want for a partner. They are familiar with the market, the suppliers, and the vendors. First they must identify the need. This should be easy if the Needs Assessment Tool (Exercise 5) was completed because the output of this assessment is the need. Once the need is clearly identified, I ask the assessment team to brainstorm a list of potential candidates to fill the need. I encourage them to build off each other's ideas and develop as comprehensive a list as possible.

The next step is to evaluate the potential of this list of candidates. Building a matrix helps you visualize how each prospect might satisfy your needs. Chart 3 profiles potential partners for a small computer firm that needs to grow to stay competitive, indicating how each one might meet a strategic need. Based on this matrix, a computer firm

Chart 3

Potential Partner Matrix

Potential Partner	Strategic Need		
	Product Development	Market Expansion	Distribution
IBM	✓		
SunComp		✓	✓
PC Products	✓	✓	✓
Lake	✓		
Nokomis	✓	✓	✓

needing to develop new products, expand its market, and secure new distribution outlets would probably want to take a closer look at PC Products and Nokomis as partnering candidates. Now that the computer firm has identified these two candidates, it needs to find out what it can offer the potential partner.

WHAT DO YOUR PARTNERS NEED FROM YOU?

If you're going to sell your potential partner on the idea of partnering, you need to know what you have to offer. It's just like a sales transaction. If there's no need, there's no sale. People do buy things they don't need, of course. But what happens after the sale? They return the product. They discount the transaction and never repeat it. The sales relationship is short-lived. If you want a good, strong partnership, it will pay you to bring your potential partners up to speed on the concept you are using to partner. You can do this by helping your potential partners identify their needs.

In the exploring stage of partnership development, your main concern is finding out what a potential partner wants. You already know what you want because you've completed the Needs Assessment Tool (Exercise 5). When you first contact a potential partner, make sure you share your information first. This will demonstrate your willingness to be open and direct. Make it clear that you're looking for an equitable partner. This engenders openness and invites the other party to disclose information.

If this potential partner expresses an interest in the possibility of working together, ask them to explain what expertise they have, where they've been, and where they'd like to go. And make sure that you listen attentively to their answers. The point is to learn what they need and how you might fulfill that need. Stick to possibilities. Don't ask for specific commitments or plans yet. If they're still interested in working together after you've exchanged some information, explain the Partnership Continuum model. Explain how the model helps people communicate effectively and provides a blueprint for creating mutually beneficial partnerships. With this tool, you can see what information you need to give and get. At the same time, it will help your potential partner communicate more easily. It will put the discussion where it belongs: in the context of partnerships.

To help you structure this discussion, fill out the Partner Compatibility Analysis (Exercise 6). With your potential partner present, ask the questions. As you listen to the answers and write down the responses, try to determine whether there is compatibility between you. Is their vision consistent with yours in terms of where you both want to go? If there's any doubt, probe deeper to ascertain whether there's enough commonality to allow for consensus between you. While you're getting information from your potential partner, you're also giving them information about yourself and where you want to go. Ask them to fill out a Partner Compatibility Analysis on you as well. After filling out the Partner Compatibility Analysis, share your findings and conclusions with the potential partner—either immediately or after consulting with top leadership.

Finding the right partner takes time. Don't be discouraged if a partner you thought would be ideal does not work out. Companies should interview at least three potential partners before selecting one. In a way, it's a lot like dating. You don't want to marry the first person you go out with. In business, you don't want to form a partnership with the first potential partner you meet. Someone better suited to your needs may come along at any moment.

A while back I worked with USWEST Communications in a major effort to create better communications between management and

Exercise 6. Partner Compatibility Analysis		
Question	Compatible? (Yes/No)	Comment/ Actions Needed
1. What is their vision?		
2. Where do they want to go as a business?		
3. What are their values and ethics?		
4. What kind of corporate culture do they have?		
5. What types of relationships and partnerships do they now have?		
6. How well have they been working?		
7. What are their strategies to achieve their vision?		
8. Have they conducted an internal assessment?		

union workers. At the outset relations were hostile, distrustful, counterproductive, and in many cases dysfunctional. Management and unions sought to form a mutually supportive partnership. But realizing even tiny steps toward that end seemed next to impossible. Our first task was to identify the "what's in it for me" part of the assessment process. Our campaign—we dubbed it "Bridging the Gaps"—lasted about two years and shaped some of the material in this book. The key lesson was this: For this proposed partnership between management and union to work, the principle of interdependence had to apply. One group dominating the other would kill the relationship. If management were ever to have a partnership with union workers, it had to find out what their needs were. Through months of research involving questionnaires, interviews, focus groups, and feedback sessions, many needs were identified, clarified, and communicated. In the same way, union members learned more about the management side of the business—about dealing with economics, competition, regulation, and shareholders. Discovering what each party needed from the other was also enlightening.

In another case, Northwest Airlines' machinists union established a "Farm Out Committee" to review any contracts Northwest contemplates offering to outside companies. Although the union doesn't insist upon doing everything itself, it negotiated with Northwest the option to bid on the business first. The union acknowledged management's need to procure resources with the best possible quality at the best price. At the same time, Northwest acknowledged the union's interest in keeping the work in-house. Marv Sandrin, leader of the machinists union, tells about a huge contract for modifying pylons on Northwest's Boeing 747 passenger jets. Sandrin explains how the union managed to rescue this business from being farmed out to an outfit in Singapore. "Pylons . . . are extremely complicated," he began. "There were things we needed to do, such as changing some work rules, to bring the costs down." They did, and they won the contract. Northwest Airlines procured the best-quality work for the best price. The partnership worked because each side understood the needs of the other, and each was willing to take a chance on partnering with the other.

In 1996, Randy McPherson entered into a partnership with Dan Gutt to start up a collision repair company. In ninety days they opened seven company-owned locations in the Twin Cities area and one in Milwaukee. By the end of this period, the CARA Company (Collision Auto Repair of America) had an asset value of $12 million. What accounts for such staggering initial success? Each man had found a good partner. Both had worked in another company that franchised body shops around the country. According to McPherson, they had the three factors essential for success: "Finding the right partner with the right skills and the right vision." Each of them knew that the other's skills were indispensable in the partnership. They also knew that their personalities seemed to mesh.

According to McPherson, "a partnership is a bridge with people working together to get from here to there. But because people change and businesses evolve, a partnership is a temporary arrangement—even if it lasts thirty years." The critical element for these two founders is their vision. "The two most devastating events in a person's life," says

McPherson, "are divorce and the death of a loved one. An automobile accident comes in third. This is why we've devised our company mission not just to fix cars, but to help people put their lives back together." Their mission statement reads: "Ease the trauma of auto accidents." I'm not aware of a more succinct message for any company. Their strategic marketing plan flows from this mission and includes ways to help customers through the trauma of auto accidents. For instance, CARA offers these services for no extra charge:

- Vehicle pickup and delivery
- Towing to a CARA shop
- Assistance in dealing with insurance companies
- Detailing after repairs are complete
- Furnishing a loan car for up to seven days if insurance doesn't provide a rental

The partners knew what they wanted, assessed their common visions and missions, and agreed on a marketing strategy for expanding their company. As their business changes and evolves, their vision and mission will give them guidance in how they should market, how they should operate, and how they should make decisions. Just as in a strong personal relationship, vows and good intentions do not guarantee faithfulness and longevity. It's the daily dedication and rededication to the partnership that counts.

The Partnership Continuum helps set expectations and facilitates communication between potential partners. As a guide and a blueprint, it's the best guarantee that an organization will arrive at its predetermined destination.

AGREEING TO PARTICIPATE

Now that you've found a partner who is compatible and willing to work with you, there has to be some type of commitment that you are going to do something together. I think of it as kind of an engagement. It is a trial period during which you can test whether you want to continue with a full partnership.

Different organizations approach the agreement to participate in different ways. Whatever the approach, the subject should be addressed in a clear and direct manner. If you're working with someone who isn't sure they want to commit, they have no incentive to help you achieve your goals. And you'll be left wondering why they refuse to commit. Are you being used? Are they just taking your information and planning to walk away? This doubt is a very destructive force in partnerships. It is the seed of mistrust. In the shadow of mistrust, the partnership will never attain the peak of synergy envisioned when the alliance was formed. Moreover, the mistrust will prevent the partnership from feeling secure enough to move into the creative zone.

I once worked for a consulting firm that was trying to partner with a big multinational's learning and organizational effectiveness center. For more than eight months we tried to finalize a scope of service agreement with this center so that we could provide consultants to teach their material. But time and again they returned this document for new stipulations or addendums. After a while, it became very clear that they weren't interested in forming a partnership with our firm at all. Their tactic, in fact, was to keep us occupied. They wanted to prevent us from using our quality training because in some ways we were their competition. They managed this by insisting on a clause in our contract stating that all contacts with businesses must be made through them. In retrospect, we realized they wanted us out of the way. After all, we were already very successful in several of their businesses. But they wanted those businesses to use *their* quality training, not ours. They had no incentive to sign an agreement with us. They did string us along, however, and our firm spent thousands of dollars jumping through hoops for nothing. We should have realized that when they were unwilling to commit, something else was going on—something that had nothing to do with partnering. The agreement to participate simply means that the partners will try one activity—one task—together and then analyze the outcome of the task-relationship dynamic to see if they want to pursue the partnership.

Now let's turn to another example. I was working with the U.S. Postal Service and its unions in forming a partnership. One of the major unions, the National Association of Letter Carriers, did not want to form a partnership with management to improve the workplace environment. While management was very disturbed by the union's refusal to get involved, I thought it was a courageous step for the union to declare its intention honestly. If the union had stayed on as an uncommitted participant, it would have found every possible way to disrupt the efforts of management. While management left the door open for the union to join the workplace environment task force, they proceeded with their work. Ultimately, I think the union missed an opportunity to serve its members. After all, management was committed—along with the other unions and professional organizations—to improving the workplace environment. But because there was no trust between this union and postal service management, the union declined to participate.

Two of the most common methods for formalizing the commitment to participate are in written format and verbal format. I prefer the first method. I think it's best to put agreements in writing, especially at the beginning of the partnership. I also think it acts as a ritual to cement the agreement. Rituals are important because they convey the organization's values and ethics. When two parties commit to participate, they are publicly acknowledging the value they place on the partnership. They are telling their employees it is important in their organizational development.

Writing down a commitment is one way of achieving this public statement. Unions and companies frequently write this commitment into their labor contracts. USWEST Communications and Communications Workers of America have established a long tradition of including letters of commitment at the beginning of their contracts to spell out why and how they intend to partner with each other. When writing out the commitment to participate, put in as many details as the partnership wishes to accomplish. Generally I encourage people to include the following:

- Reasons why partnering is important to both parties
- The scope of the commitment (quality improvement, marketing, supplier/customer benefit, sales, or distribution)
- The duration of the commitment (one project; one year; until we mutually agree to quit)
- Expected benefits from the partnership (better product distribution; more access to technology)

I am less optimistic about partners who give only a verbal commitment unless there's a history of trust between them. Too often partners who are unwilling to commit formally are not ready to be good partners. The commitment to participate indicates that partners have increased their partnering intelligence—their PQ—enough to risk the pain of failure for the opportunity and benefits only true partnering can provide.

The exploring stage is exciting but also anxiety producing. It is exciting because of the limitless opportunities available to us. It is anxiety producing because people are being asked to make a commitment. It is during the exploring stage that you may encounter your first partnering conflict. You have begun to examine each other's material and ethereal realms. This means you not only are looking at each other's material production to determine whether there are complementary synergies, but you've started to look at each other's vision, values, culture, and ethics. While exploring, certain comments or questions may give rise to negative or conflicting feelings. In this early stage, care must be taken to ensure that any conflicts that arise are resolved in a win-win manner. This first encounter with conflict will set the mental maps for what happens in the future.

Partners are being asked to take a stand. At this point, people want to begin defining how the partnership will affect them. Since the idea is still an unknown quantity, many will feel anxious and insecure. This is a good time to begin practicing some of the partnering skills. Think about the six PQ attributes. Examine your personal feelings about the unknown. Explore your vision of the future. Talk about the changes and ask for insights into what will build trust between the partners and help you feel confident about the commitment.

EXPLORING STAGE
PLAN–DO–CHECK–ACT CYCLE

You have decided that you are ready to incorporate the strategy of partnering to help you achieve your goals. You understand, having conducted a systemic needs assessment, how the organization's vision, values, ethics, and culture affect its mission, strategies, processes, products, and services. Now it is time to go exploring for a potential partner. This chapter has presented the steps and tools for identifying and assessing partners. You can build quality into the process by using the Plan–Do–Check–Act cycle of continuous improvement. This is accomplished by listing the tasks that need to occur in the Exploring Stage under each step of the Plan–Do–Check–Act cycle. On the following pages, I have put together a sample of what to do in each step. You may want to use this sample as is or modify it to meet your particular objectives. Either way, it will help you accomplish the task in less time and with greater efficiency and higher quality.

PLAN

The first step is to determine the type of partnership you want. Ask yourself the following questions. To close the gaps I identified in the Needs Assessment Tool (Exercise 5):

- Do I have a natural partnership?
- Do I need to partner internally before partnering externally?
- Do I need technical, distribution, marketing, development, sales, or other expertise?
- Do I have a partnership with my employees or their union?

Now that you have determined the type of partnership you need in order to close the gap, make sure that you're clear about the need you want your partnership to fill.

Brainstorm a list of potential partners who could fill your need best. Complete the Potential Partner Matrix (Chart 3) to help you narrow your list of potential partners. Determine the criteria you'll use to identify these partners. Once the potential partners have been identified, think about how you want to approach your partner to ask for a commitment. In general, it's best to come right out and ask for the commitment. If your partner is ready, he or she will already be thinking about the partnership and will be grateful you popped the question.

Then determine together how you want to formalize the commitment to participate. However you choose to formalize the commitment, be sure to use consensus and develop the commitment together. Here are some items you may want to include in the commitment:

- Scope of the commitment
- Duration of the commitment
- Activities to be included
- Contributions to be made
- Governance of the partnership
- Management of the partnership
- Signatory page

DO

Contact your list of potential partners. Ask to set up a meeting with them. Tell them what you are hoping to accomplish. I encourage my clients to be as straightforward as possible. Remember: How we act in the initial meeting will form the mental map our partner will carry for some time to come. Tell the potential partner what you need. Explain how you think you can work together to fill that need. Ask them about their needs and discuss whether you are in a position to satisfy them. It could be as basic as this: "I'm a manufacturer and need a product to sell. You have a retail business and want products that will draw customers." It's not complicated. Getting down to basics helps identify the core needs of each partner and clearly shows how the strategy of partnering can help both parties achieve their goals.

After you've interviewed all your potential partners, complete the Partner Compatibility Analysis (Exercise 6). What does this tell you? Is there one potential partner who meets more of your requirements than others? Are there no potential partners? Do you need to go out and look for others to interview? Using the Plan–Do–Check–Act cycle, continue to contact and review potential partners until you've found one who meets all of your criteria. Once you have identified them, you need to ask whether they view the partnership as a mutually beneficial idea. Can they commit to engaging in the initial activity with you?

CHECK

After you have completed the Partner Compatibility Analysis (Exercise 6), you are ready to enter the plan stage of the Plan–Do–Check–Act cycle again. The question then becomes what do you plan for? Do you need to discover more partners? Can you select a partner from the present list? Do you need to go back and interview some of the prospective partners again because some clarifying questions may have been introduced? Regardless of the outcome of this step, go back to the plan step of the cycle to complete this stage of the process.

Once you've selected your partner and have agreed to participate in an initial activity, it's time to do a process observation check with each other. How did your process work? Are you both feeling good about how you formalized the commitment to participate? Did the exercise build trust between you? Did you communicate well with each other? Was each party open and direct?

ACT

If you are satisfied with the commitment to participate, you are now ready to move to the next stage in the Partnership Continuum: initiating. If you're not satisfied, you need to plan the next step. Do you want to approach the partner again and address the commitment to participate? Or should you go back to the exploring stage and look for a different partner?

INTERNAL PARTNERSHIP: CONVENTION HOTEL

Marty and Jean knew they needed to work together to make their vision a reality. There was no question of working with other partners. This was an internal partnership. But they needed to explore their compatibility. So as a team-building exercise to help them begin thinking about how their relationship might develop, I asked them to complete the Partner Compatibility Analysis (Exercise 5). Marty balked. "Look, I know that I have to work with Jean, and I think we've identified the scheduling as one area we can work on. But I don't want to waste my time with that compatibility thing. Can't we just move on?" Jean replied: "Let's just look at it, Marty. It might help." So look at it we did. After a few minutes they started answering the questions out loud, so I suggested we just informally capture on paper what they were saying. Neither objected, and their compatibility analysis (see p. 102) is what we came up with. Marty and Jean noticed they both answered no in areas that concerned their relationships. They vowed this was one area they were going to work on.

EXTERNAL PARTNERSHIP: DOWNTOWN OFFICE TOWER

The second meeting was set up a week after all the requests for pricing had been submitted. Each response had its pluses and minuses. While most of the nonunion bids were slightly less in monetary cost, they had certain negative components. For example, the plumbing contractor could not provide the number of skilled plumbers needed just when the project would most require their skill. The heating and cooling contractor cost pennies less than its union counterpart but had fewer licensed specialists on its payroll. The union contractors came in with bids that met all the special requirements and certifications needed, but they were slightly higher in labor cost. After reviewing the bids, John told Peter he'd like to go with the union contractors if the union would lower its cost by 2 cents per labor hour. That would make the union contractors' bids economically competitive with nonunion labor. Peter thought the job would hire enough skilled labor to make the project worthwhile, so he'd ask the locals to enact their Market Recovery Program funds to apply toward labor costs. (This is a fund union members pay into to make their labor cost more competitive when bidding against nonunion contractors.) In this case labor costs were close. But labor could offer something the nonunion contractors couldn't, and John knew this.

The following week they met again. Peter had met with the labor council and brought a proposal back to John. "John, the labor costs on this project are very close. We'll subsidize the labor cost 1 cent per labor

Jean and Marty's Partner Compatibility Analysis

Question	Compatible? (Yes/No)	Comment/ Actions Needed
1. What is their vision? *Answer: Mutually developed a vision statement.*	Yes	*"Each guest would have a clean room in which everything worked properly."*
2. Where do they want to go as a business? *Answer: Both want to be successful in their respective areas.*	Yes	
3. What are their values and ethics? *Answer: Both agree that they want to provide an excellent guest experience—and the condition of the room contributes to that.*	Yes	*Marty: Just getting the job done quickly is important. Jean: Making sure everything is completed properly is important.*
4. What kind of corporate culture do they have? *Answer: Supportive of teamwork.*	Yes	
5. What types of relationships and partnerships do they now have? *Answer: They are suspicious of each other. There is low trust and they blame each other for the problem. Marty acknowledges he finds it difficult to work with others. Jean feels that Marty does not respect her.*	No	
6. How well have they been working? *Answer: Both agree they have had no partnership together in the past.*	No	
7. What are their strategies to achieve their vision? *Answer: They would like to work together to identify where they can help each other achieve their respective goals.*	Yes	
8. Have they conducted an internal assessment? *Answer: They have not conducted a formal needs assessment, but they know the extent of the problem and have some ideas on solutions.*	Yes	*Marty: Needs to work on developing the stages of relationship. Jean: Wants to understand the complexities of Marty's tasks.*

hour. But if we do this, we want you to sign a project agreement with us. As you know, in a project agreement we'll ensure that you have the needed labor and we'll provide you with a no-strike clause. And in return you'll agree to make this an all-union work site. Additionally, we'll help reduce the labor cost to make the job cost-competitive with nonunion contractors. Your client needs to have this job completed on time. Going with a nonunion contractor opens you up to risk in this area. Our record proves that if you sign a project agreement with us, you won't be held up by labor problems. Will you commit to a project agreement?"

John thought about it for a few minutes. While the labor would cost slightly more than he wanted, he knew Peter was right about getting the job completed on time. The trades had the resources needed to complete the job. With nonunion contractors, some were excellent but getting enough people on site was always an issue. John asked Peter: "What would I need to do if I were to commit to using all-union labor on this project?" Peter suggested they review a Project Partnering Agreement that the Building and Construction Council had used on other projects. Then, they could decide what to include in or exclude from their agreement. John liked the idea, so they proceeded. The Project Partnering Agreement that Peter showed him was five pages long and included thirteen articles. Each article addressed a term of the agreement. John took a minute to review each section. He liked what he saw:

Project Partnering Agreement

Article I. Declaration of Policy

This agreement is entered into for the purpose of ensuring that the work on the project may proceed without strikes, stoppages, slowdowns, or interruptions and that the project is a credit to the civil responsibility of the building industry. It is agreed that harmonious labor-management relations are the result of responsible conduct by the building trades and the contractor's management personnel. It is our mutual desire to promote these relationships on the project as an expression of responsibility and good faith toward the community and the industry.

Article II. Definitions

This article defined the following words in order to clear up any ambiguity:
- **Construction work**
- **Life of the project**
- **Employer and employers**
- **Employee**
- **Unions or union**

Article III. Scope of Agreement

This article identified the scope of the agreement and affirmed that its term was for the life of the project, that it did not apply to management or professional roles, and that it did not supersede existing collective bargaining agreements.

Article IV. No Strike, No Lockout

This article stated that the union would not strike the work site and management would not lock out employees in case of a disagreement.

Article V. Construction Work Contract Requirements

This article stated that union contractors with collective bargaining agreements would carry out all construction work. Then it defined the meaning of "construction work," such as demolition, trucking, and signage. Another paragraph addressed failure to comply with this article of the agreement and how it would be resolved.

Article VI. Trust Fund Payments

This paragraph discussed how the contractor would pay into the union trust fund to provide benefits for workers.

Article VII. Effect of Agreement

This article affirmed that by signing this agreement, both partners agreed to its terms.

Article VIII. Union Access to Project

This article ensured that authorized union representatives had access to the project site.

Article IX. Management of Project

This article affirmed management's right to manage the project in accordance with local union agreements.

Article X. Pre-Job Conference

This article stated that the union and management would meet before the project commenced to discuss all anticipated work assignments and work out communications and problem-solving techniques.

Article XI. Jurisdictional Disputes

This article affirmed that no project work would cease due to jurisdictional disputes between unions and that such disputes would be resolved in accordance with the plan for settlement of jurisdictional disputes in the construction industry guidelines.

Article XII. General Clause

This article stated that all terms and conditions not set out in this agreement would be prescribed by the applicable union contract.

Article XIII. Successor Clause

This article affirmed the right of any succeeding organization to assume the agreement.

Signatures⎯⎯⎯⎯⎯⎯⎯⎯⎯⎯⎯⎯⎯   ⎯⎯⎯⎯⎯⎯⎯⎯⎯⎯⎯⎯⎯⎯⎯⎯

John thought the agreement looked pretty good as it was, but he wanted to take it back to his firm's legal department and have it verified. Peter agreed and asked John if he thought they had a partnership. John smiled and said: "Barring any unforeseen difficulties, I think this is a go!" They agreed to meet in two days to sign the Project Partnering Agreement.

CHAPTER SIX

Initiating Stage

Reaping the Benefits of Partnership

On February 8, 1998, National Public Radio carried a feature story about the troubles of the final American astronaut aboard the MIR space station. Andy Thomas, from NASA, apparently had not learned to speak Russian very well—a failing that had caused friction with the cosmonauts on board and had been widely reported in Russian newspapers. In a press conference, a testy Russian journalist asked Andy Thomas, "How are you becoming accommodated to the station? Please answer in Russian."

Tensions can build up even among people who have well-defined common missions, exceptionally rigorous training, and common exposure in the most public fishbowl imaginable. Dr. Vadim Gushen, a Russian space psychologist quoted on the radio program, explained that the astronauts do receive one year to eighteen months' language training at a school in Moscow. They learn all the technical and procedural words and phrases they need to do their jobs. But he maintains they need much more: "Some astronauts don't progress beyond operational language, but they should. They are not only working there but also living there. It's not just a matter of your technical knowledge, but talk about life, about your social side. If you can't talk about what you're feeling, you're severely restricted." The narrator went on to explain that Shannon Lucid, who spent six months on MIR in 1996, did well because she spent time fitting in with her group. Gushen commented: "Her first priority was the social side. Whenever she had to choose, she chose to communicate with the social side."

When we translate this into the context of PQ, it demonstrates in a dramatic way that you can't focus solely on the task. There has to be a balance between the task and relationship components of the partnership. People with a high PQ understand this balance and are able to increase their proficiency in both areas. Moreover, the personal dynamics of the relationships on board MIR may hold some lessons for future space missions, such as the International Space Station to be built in the next decade. Not only will there be representatives from different nations living together for prolonged periods, but there will be more diverse mixes of people: male and female, scientists and non-scientists, military and civilian, old and young, and individuals of different races, religions, and socioeconomic backgrounds.

According to other social scientists who commented on this story, the intense isolation, lack of personal space, and constant stress of a mission can result in dysfunctional dynamics. Miscommunication, negative social dynamics, and the formation of cliques may threaten a mission's success. The language issue points to some critical problems we must face in any partnership. Business partnerships face many conflicts and pressures, not the least of which is the issue of blending entire workforces and cultures together. The reporter closed his story with these remarks: "Cliques and language barriers are only symptoms. The real problem is crew members getting to know each other on Earth, before they confront the stresses of space. Team members need to know about your family, friends, interests, and humor. A lack of such knowledge causes a lack of trust."

PREPARING TO ACT

I see a clear parallel with business partnerships. The time we spend getting to know our partners will pay off in terms of more trust, less friction, and more productivity in the end. In the initiating stage, we can plan to limit pressure by negotiating realistic timelines and defining ahead of time how we'll measure our success. We'll clarify what we want from each other up front, and we'll agree on our partnership mission. Like the astronauts, we'll be clear about what tasks we need to perform. But we'll also commit to developing the relationship with our partner as a prerequisite for success.

In the initiating stage, we're starting to move away from planning our partnership and toward activities we created the partnership to accomplish. In other words, now we are ready to start a task.

When initiating your partnership, it is important to remember to keep the task and relationship activities balanced. Let's revisit for a moment Figure 4 on page 57, Timeline for a Successful Partnership. Up front, in the first trimester of development, you want to spend about two-thirds of your time on relationship development and about one-third on task design. This is also true once you have identified your partner and are initiating an activity. It is important to build the relationship with the partnering team that implements the initial activity. Spending the time up front will result in exponential benefits in the end. The challenge at this step is to build a strong relationship between the partners while creating a plan for a successful task.

Building a partnership always takes longer than people anticipate. Therefore, you need to plan time for relationship development. Conduct a team-building exercise to cement the relationship. Focus the team-building session on the task-relationship dynamics. Make planning the task a part of the team-building activity. You'll be amazed at how well this technique works.

Make sure key leadership is present to kick off the initial activity. When key leadership is visible, the partnering activities are generally more successful. When key leadership is absent, it sends the nonverbal message "This is not important." Plan a launch. Invite people in the organizations to witness the kickoff. Write articles in the employee newsletters and provide media releases. Send the message, "This is important! You are partnering with another business and you can look for these benefits."

Make sure everyone knows the partnership's vision and goals. Keep this information in the forefront of people's minds. One sure way to kill a partnership is to be ambiguous or miscommunicate the purpose and goals for the partnership. Also, be sure to inform people when the goals change or are updated.

Gather support for the partnership from the organization's employees. Keep the employees informed about what's going on and why it is occurring. Point out how the partnership will benefit the organization. Talk about how it will provide job security by increasing marketing capabilities, opportunities for product distribution, and technological innovation. The employees need to support the partnership for it to be successful.

Once the partnering team for the initial activity has been selected, it is important to choose an initial project that creates a win-win outcome for all parties and has a good chance of success. An example of such a project took place in Washington, D.C. The city government was in a state of chaos. Among the more evident symptoms was its inability to replace damaged and vandalized parking meters within a reasonably quick time frame. The city was losing thousands of dollars a day in revenue since people couldn't drop coins into the meters. In an excellent example of a public-private partnership, the city of Washington, D.C., formed an alliance with Lockheed Martin IMS to remedy the situation. Lockheed Martin IMS agreed to take over maintaining and replacing city parking meters. In exchange, the city agreed to give Lockheed Martin a percentage of the total revenue collected. Each party won. Parking meter revenue began to increase and the city's image began to improve as the public perception of meter care improved. Things looked less run-down, better cared for. Lockheed Martin began to turn a small profit in the deal and was assured of continued city contracts.

In addition to building a healthy foundation through developing trustworthy relationships, one of the most important tasks of the partnering team is assessing the level of contribution each partner provides to the overall success of the project. While each member of the alliance has completed an internal assessment identifying its own needs and learned how it can help satisfy its partner's needs, it is during the initial activity that the whole puzzle comes together. It is at this stage that each member begins to realize how its individual contributions are turned from proposed benefits into tangible assets. This is accomplished by bringing the partnering team together and designing a plan to complete a task.

Bringing Together the Partnering Team

To begin the initial activity process, assemble the team that will be responsible for implementing the activity. Once the team is together, review Exercise 7, the Initial Activity Team Checklist I have developed for use during the team-building and planning session. This session will probably take place over a period of days or even weeks, depending on the scope of the activity.

This checklist covers both the stages of relationship development and the stages of partnership development. In the initial meeting it is important to spend time on developing the relationship. Note, however, that people will want to move right to task. It is important that they understand that by establishing the relationship issues first, they will save time in the long run. Ultimately, when people go directly to task, relationship issues impede task development, causing conflict and frustration.

Exercise 7. Initial Activity Team Checklist

Stages of Relationship Development

Activity	Desired Outcome for Partner 1	Desired Outcome for Partner 2	Agreements
Have all sides agreed on the partnership?			
Is everyone here voluntarily?			
What is our initial activity?			
Do we agree on a common vision for the initial activity?			
Have we established our ethical standards?			
How will we decide leadership issues?			
How will decisions be made regarding the partnership?			
What are our norms of behavior during the time we are acting in partnership?			
What do we expect from each partner in this relationship?			
What do we need to receive from each partner in this relationship?			
How will we resolve differences?			
What is the preferred method of resolving conflicts?			
How will we resolve problems?			

Exercise 7. Initial Activity Team Checklist continued

Stages of Partnership Development

Activity	Desired Outcome for Partner 1	Desired Outcome for Partner 2	Agreements
What is our method of communication between us?			
Between our sponsors and us?			
Between the greater organizations and us?			
What level of information do we agree to share?			
What information, if any, is off-limits?			
How will we provide each other with feedback?			
How will we self-disclose information to each other?			
What does trust look like to us?			
How will we manage a situation in which mistrust exists?			
How will we manage change?			
How will we manage to maintain equality between partners?			
How will we measure the development of our relationship?			
How do we move from independence to interdependence?			
How will we know when to call it quits?			

Exercise 7. Initial Activity Team Checklist continued

Stages of Partnership Development

Activity	Desired Outcome for Partner 1	Desired Outcome for Partner 2	Agreements
What is the initial activity?			
What is the scope of the activity?			
Identify the benefits for this activity for each partner. Tangible? Intangible?			
What are the start and stop points?			
When will we know the activity is complete?			
What impacts will the partnership have on each organization's culture?			
What strategies are in place to define what we will accomplish?			
How do these strategies link back to the sponsoring partner's organizational strategies?			
What impacts does the partnership have on the sponsoring organization's annual and long-term strategic plan?			
What is the time frame for the overall initial activity?			
What is the timeline for the specific project?			
What is the time impact on the initial activity team?			
What impacts does the partnership have on the timing of other strategic issues in the greater organizations?			

Exercise 7. Initial Activity Team Checklist continued

Stages of Partnership Development

Activity	Desired Outcome for Partner 1	Desired Outcome for Partner 2	Agreements
What are the processes we will be impacting/ developing?			
Where are those processes located?			
Who currently owns those processes?			
Are those processes capable of accomplishing our objectives?			
What resources are needed to update or reengineer the existing processes?			
What level of contribution does each partner provide?			
Is the contribution direct or indirect?			
How do we share the rewards?			
How do we share the risks?			
How will we benchmark our activities?			
Who else out there is doing this or something like this?			
How will we measure the success of the activity?			
How will we measure return based on contribution?			
Can the level of contribution be isolated or determined based on percentage of return?			

Exercise 7. Initial Activity Team Checklist continued

Stages of Partnership Development

Activity	Desired Outcome for Partner 1	Desired Outcome for Partner 2	Agreements
What resources are needed to accomplish the project?			
Who provides what resources and at what level?			
What skills are required to operate and manage the new activities?			
Do we have the skill set available or do we need to attain it?			
What type of training will be required to manage the new processes?			
How do we trade resources to get the skills needed?			
How are the joint processes managed once the activity is under way?			
How will we communicate the impacts of the activity on the greater organizations?			
Once the activity has started, what plans are in place to close unforeseen gaps?			
How are innovations developed in the alliance to be handled?			
How will we maintain a relative balance between the partners?			
How will we measure the balance?			

How to Use the Initial Activity Team Checklist

Once the team is assembled, begin with the Stages of Partnership Development section. I ask each partner or team of partners from the same organization to fill out their column separately. Then, after each team has had this opportunity, we discuss each partner's response until we reach an agreement. This takes time. It may move slowly at first, but this is time well invested in the development of what may be a huge portion of your business. Please note: Although this example lists only two partners, if there are more than two you will want to make sure each group involved is provided with input and feedback. Continue until all the items have been resolved. You then have the foundation to develop your project plan.

INITIATING STAGE
PLAN–DO–CHECK–ACT CYCLE

You think you have found the ideal partner. You want to know if this is the right partner before you invest too much time, money, and resources in the alliance. You have assembled the partnering team. You are ready to try the initial activity. Review the steps and tools in Chapter 6 for starting the initial activity. You can build quality into the process by using the Plan–Do–Check–Act cycle of continuous improvement. This can be accomplished by listing the tasks that need to occur in the Initiating Stage below each step of the Plan–Do–Check–Act cycle. On the following pages, I have put together a sample of what to do in each step. You may want to use this example as is or modify it to meet your particular objectives. Either way, it will help you accomplish the task in less time and with greater efficiency and higher quality.

PLAN

To accomplish a task successfully, the first thing the partners should do is sit down and plan what it is they are going to do. The Initial Activity Team Checklist (see Exercise 7) and the Agreement Between Partners Checklist (see Chart 4) will help them remember key items. I like checklists. Pilots, regardless of the number of hours they have logged on a certain type of aircraft, always use a preflight checklist before taking off. It's wise to do the same with any important activity—and the initial activity in a partnership falls into the category of "important activities" for me. After all, you've spent time, energy, and money to identify your needs and find a partner.

You'll want to give the initial activity as much of a chance of success as possible. falls into the category of "important activities" for me. After all, you've spent time, energy, and money to identify your needs and find a partner. When you use these checklists, you and your partner must work together and, using consensus, talk through the issues. I recommend that you write down your agreements—not to use them as a club should things go wrong, but to clarify issues as the planning proceeds.

Sometime during the initial activity or immediately after, set a meeting to discuss with everyone involved how well the partnership is working. The key document you'll want to review is the Agreement Between Partners Checklist (Chart 4). You'll also want to address the relationship issues. Select one or more of the tools (the Partners' Trust Questionnaire and/or the Partnership Stressor Checklist) to assess the stages of relationship development. Be sure the agenda you send out in advance has been written or approved by the partners.

Chart 4

Agreement Between Partners Checklist

- ❑ Define the area of interest where we are going to create an initial activity (marketing, sales, product development, and so forth). Brainstorm a list of potential activities we can do together. Can we agree on one specific activity to work on together?
- ❑ Document the start and stop point of the activity. Develop a timeline of the activity. Set the boundaries of the activity (what we won't try to accomplish).
- ❑ List the various roles and responsibilities of each partner.
- ❑ Agree on the decision-making style to be used.
- ❑ Gain consensus on the strategy for resolving conflict.
- ❑ Allocate resource contributions and commitments in writing.
- ❑ Create a set of criteria to evaluate the success or failure of the task objectives.
- ❑ Create a set of criteria to evaluate the success of the relationship development.
- ❑ Define the expected outcomes of the initial activity.

DO

Complete a project together. Sort of like a first date, planning initial activities with a partner enables us to work together without the pressure of eternal commitment. We don't have to prove we are ideal mates. We also avoid jumping into a relationship that presumes we will do more than we want to do. The planning reduces the risk of unrealistic expectations.

Just by working through the "preflight" checklist, you communicate to your partner that you have certain expectations. When you embark on a *planned* adventure, you've already influenced some of the dynamics of the trip. Spontaneity is replaced by planfulness, which opens the way for communication and sets expectations for both partners. After you've completed the project, it's time for a debriefing (see Chart 5).

CHECK

By establishing a trial project with both task and relationship objectives, you have specified the performance you expect from each other. Based on the criteria, rating system, or measurements you established in the first phase with the Agreement Between Partners Checklist, the results of the initial activity should be obvious. If you set a goal of opening ten stores in ninety days, for example, and you're now looking back after ninety days, you can measure your progress quantitatively. If you set a short-term goal of developing a joint marketing strategy as measured by a written marketing plan you both embrace, you can measure your progress by that evidence. You'll also want to talk about the stages of relationship development:

- What did we do to move us out of the forming stage?
- How well did we manage our conflict during the storming stage?
- What sort of norms have we developed?
- What value-added outcome was achieved in the performing stage?

Again, you need to strike a balance between task and relationship development every step of the way. You don't want to start taking each other for granted, especially after your first activity together.

I know this will be hard for many in business. My experience tells me managers do not want to sit around and "waste their time" talking about relationships. But this is a critical investment and you may have thousands—or even millions—of dollars riding on the success of your partnership. So it's absolutely essential to discuss the relationship issues with your partner.

In evaluating your initial activity, of course, you'll also want to identify new information you didn't have before. You'll want to look at other

Chart 5

Debriefing the Initial Activity

After the initial activity is completed, begin to evaluate its outcome. Invite your partner to a debriefing meeting. During this meeting, split your time roughly 50/50 and discuss both the stages of partnership development and the stages of relationship development. Ask the following questions:

Stages of Partnership Development

- What was the outcome of the first activity?
- Did you accomplish what you expected?
- Did the plan work as expected?
- What did you learn from the activity?
- What surprised you about the activity?
- Did working in partnership create any breakthroughs?

Then talk about the relationship. When discussing the stages of relationship development, ask the following questions:

Stages of Relationship Development

- Did you find balance in the task/relationship components?
- How did you cope with the change created by the initial activity?
- Did you build trust? How do you know?
- How did you manage your conflict?
- Can you give specific examples of conflict that was resolved using a win-win solution?
- Did the partners create a sense of interdependence—that is, did you rely on each other for success?
- How did you do in self-disclosure?
- Did you give your partner feedback? Did you receive feedback?
- How did the flow of information work?
- What type of information did you share?
- Did the information sharing create any breakthroughs?
- Did anything happen that you didn't expect?
- What was it?

opportunities and synergies your partnership suggests. You'll also want to account for problems or breakdowns in the process. You'll want to use this stage as a learning opportunity, not just a "pass/fail" appraisal.

At the end of the meeting you might want to list what I call the "pluses and deltas." The "pluses" are things that worked well in the meeting. The "deltas" are the items you'd like to have changed for the next meeting. If you or your partner are having trouble in any of the six attributes—past/future orientation, comfort with change, and the like—you'll want to turn to Part Two of the book and review the attribute that's causing you difficulty. There you'll find skill-building exercises and surveys you can take to help you increase your partnering intelligence in each attribute.

ACT

With your new insights and real-world data of how you performed together, you now have three options. The first is to abandon the partnership effort. If the initial activity proved too painful, unproductive, stressful, or disappointing, you should have the intelligence to abandon the effort, cut your losses, and look for more promising opportunities. This is not necessarily a tragic event. After all, it's better to know early on that the partnership will not bear fruit.

Second, partners can take the information they have, redesign their next activity together, and try it again. Using the Plan–Do–Check–Act cycle, you can return to the planning stage and devise more activities. Partners who still want to work together can revise goals, adjust responsibilities, or redouble their efforts to accomplish worthwhile goals together.

Third, you can move on to greater investment—that is, more substantial commitment to the partnership. Assuming the initial activities confirmed expectations—that both task and relationship objectives were satisfied—why not move ahead? The next phases of activity should build on the initial successes. The Plan–Do–Check–Act cycle is reiterative: It repeats again and again. You can manage continuous progress by using good planning and good feedback systems.

Are you ready to commit to a full partnership? Or do you need to go back and rethink the partnership? The outcome of this meeting will tell you if your partnership is going to work or not. You have accomplished a thoughtful step-by-step approach to creating your partnership. Now you need to decide: Are we going to continue? Do we need to go back and rethink? Or is this it?

INTERNAL PARTNERSHIP: CONVENTION HOTEL

Marty and Jean are committed to working together and have filled out the Partner Compatibility Analysis. Since they knew they *needed* to do this, they didn't formalize their commitment to participate but simply verbalized their commitment to each other. As a next step, Jean and Marty agreed to fill out the Agreement Between Partners Checklist (Chart 4). They filled out the checklist like this:

I. We are going to coordinate the activities between housekeeping and maintenance to minimize extra work for both groups and yet attain our vision: Each guest will have a clean room in which everything works properly. We are going to review schedules. We are going to establish a process in which maintenance work will take place before the rooms are cleaned. We are going to work on building a good relationship between the maintenance and housekeeping staff.

II. We have created a timeline for: reviewing the scheduling of rooms for maintenance; reviewing the scheduling of rooms for housekeeping; developing a daily list of rooms needing maintenance; coordinating the maintenance and housekeeping staff rounds.

III. We feel that our role is to coordinate the scheduling of the rooms that require maintenance and act as go-betweens for our staffs.

IV. We agreed to use consensus as our decision-making style.

V. We both agree to work on conflict. We agree that when we have an issue between our departments, rather than go to Eric, we will go to each other and problem-solve using a win-win technique.

VI. We both agree that no additional resources are required.

VII. The measurement that we will put in place is a weekly report of the number of rooms that were cleaned before maintenance took place.

VIII. We've decided we will know how the relationship is working by using two criteria: the number of times we meet each week (the more the better) and how many times we have unresolved conflicts that require us to go to the general manager.

IX. We would be satisfied if we saw a decline in the number of complaints from customers about rooms that were not properly cleaned because of maintenance work.

After thirty days of working at their partnership, Jean and Marty wanted to review the outcome. They held a meeting with me, and the first item we reviewed was the stages of partnership development. Then Marty and Jean analyzed the data they had collected. Over the thirty days there had been more than 240 maintenance calls. During that period, all but thirteen of them had been scheduled during the normal business hours. They had been able to schedule all but three of the maintenance jobs before the rooms were cleaned. They thought this was a huge success—

especially since no guests complained about the condition of their room after a maintenance call.

Then we talked about the stages of relationship development. The criteria they established for determining the health of their relationship were the number of times they met and the number of unresolved conflicts that needed to go to the general manager. Clearly they had increased the number of times they met. They were meeting at least once a day in the morning to talk about the schedules, and sometimes they met more than once a day. They also agreed that all of their conflicts had been resolved in a win-win manner. They gave me an example: At one point, a housekeeper and a maintenance person quarreled over who was to be in the room. The housekeeper was upset because it was the last room on her shift and she wanted to pick up her child at daycare. The maintenance man needed to change the air conditioner compressor, a messy job that would take more than an hour. Jean managed to reassign the room to a housekeeper who worked a later schedule. The housekeeper was happy because she could leave; the maintenance man was happy because he could get the job done and then have the room serviced.

EXTERNAL PARTNERSHIP: DOWNTOWN OFFICE TOWER

Now that the Project Partnering Agreement was signed, John and Peter decided they wanted to monitor it to ensure compliance. In the agreement they had established a prejob conference. They invited all the subcontractors to this meeting and explained how they would measure the success of the Project Partnering Agreement. They were interested in knowing if there were any violations of the terms of the agreement. They were also interested in knowing if there were any trends among subcontractors who agreed to abide by the terms of the agreement. So they established the following chart:

Subcontractor	Date	Violation	Resolution
Twin Town Demolition			
North Star Trucking			
Gridiron Works			
All-State Heating & Cooling			
Settin Concrete Co.			
Bright Electrical Contractors			
Flush Plumbing			

John and Peter agreed to review the chart with all the subcontractors twice a year during the course of the project. Since they were expecting this project would take three years to complete, they would have six semiannual reviews.

The first piece of work completed was the demolition and removal of an old abandoned structure. They met after that segment of the project was completed to see how well the subcontractors were complying with the agreement.

Subcontractor	Date	Violation	Resolution
Twin Town Demolition	6/14/96	Nonunion Crane	Assigned crane operator was sick; will ensure all replacement operators carry current union cards.
North Star Trucking		None	

While this meeting was not without violation, the one minor infraction appeared to be due to an oversight rather than intentional. Both Peter and John felt the matter was handled appropriately and decided this was not a violation of their trust. Both thought the Project Partnering Agreement was working well and agreed to continue to monitor the results. John made a comment that seemed to sum up their success so far: "Although we've just started the project, we're already a week ahead of schedule because the demolition and site cleanup went so smoothly."

CHAPTER SEVEN

Committing Stage

Formalizing the Commitment

Everything you've done up to this point has been focused on getting you to the full partnership stage. You and your partner have worked hard together, navigating the stages of relationship development, so that there's trust and mutual benefits. And, as well, you've engaged in the steps necessary to accomplish a task in order to determine the partnership's worth to both of you. You've used the Plan–Do–Check–Act cycle to continuously improve the task and relationship dynamics of your partnership. You've seen the partnership move from a past to a future orientation.

The next two steps will feel almost anticlimactic. This is a good thing. You've worked so hard to increase your partnering intelligence that by the time you're prepared to make a commitment and move to full partnership it will feel like the only logical step. Once you've made the commitment to partnership, the only thing that stands between you and full partnership is one more task: to conduct a joint strategic planning session in order to solidify your future vision and spell out the plans to get you there. Your partnership is now in the *committing* stage. You have achieved the trust and communication needed to help you maximize the synergy. You have identified the mutual benefits that the partnership provides. Having managed the changing dynamics of the relationship and its impact on the organizations, you are now positioned to perform.

Reaching the committing stage of partnership development is the gold medal of partnering. It is the stage when "me" becomes "we." As you link your success to each other's well-being, you move from independence to interdependence. This goal is elusive for most business partnerships. While it is sometimes attained in our personal relations, few businesses achieve this stage. This doesn't mean it can't happen, but long-term partnerships are rare. Businesses change, marketplace realities evolve, and alliances shift market forces in different directions. To achieve this level of partnership ensures that so long as the partnership provides mutual benefits and trust exists, abundance will flow.

The partnership becomes institutionalized when there is formal commitment to it. In our personal lives, we have weddings or other commitment ceremonies to publicly acknowledge our partnerships. Aside from the ritual, which is important, it sends a message to the outside world that "we are in this together." United Airlines recently ran a series of advertisements featuring their employees, who had just signed an employee-ownership contract with management. The message was obvious: Since they were now owner-employees, their customers could expect service as if it were coming from the boss himself—because it was! The real message behind this commitment, however, was that owners and employees had formed a partnership and customers could expect better service from them. In an extremely competitive marketplace, this is a powerful message.

MUTUAL STRATEGIC PLANNING

Now that you've formalized your partnership, start planning for the future. Strategic planning is the best way for partners to envision what will happen in the next few years. Since you are now in a position to capitalize on the partnership, it's important to plan out together, strategically, what you want to do and how you intend to do it. When partners plan together strategically, the synergy created is enormous. And the outcome is something your competitors can't replicate because it exists only in the context of your partnership. No matter how hard they try, they cannot re-create that unique set of dynamics that are uniquely yours.

Recently I witnessed an example of this type of synergy being created through a partnership. At the time, I was participating in a workshop between a state road department and an automobile manufacturer. This multimember partnership consists of people dedicated to increasing auto safety and using technology to improve efficiencies. Their vision is to create a system whereby the automobile/road interaction enhances the car's safety and performance. This partnership is trying to design a car that will interact with information embedded in the road surface. Sensors in the road will monitor traffic, surface conditions, and other useful information and relay it to the driver via a computer. Projected onto a dashboard monitor or onto the windshield, the data will inform the driver of road conditions—dry, icy, slick, and so forth—and also signal the optimum speed the car should be traveling under these conditions. Such a system could also indicate detours, alternate routes should there be traffic delays, and so forth.

Sound like Flash Gordon or *Star Wars?* It isn't. It is the synergistic result of a partnership formed by the National Highway Safety Board, the California Department of Transportation, several automobile manufacturers, and some computer and software designers. Each of these partners had separate needs that they could not fulfill themselves. Working together, however, they are now at the point of strategically planning how they want to develop the highways and cars of the future. The first thing they did was create a vision reflecting the individual aspirations of the partners. Each had a part to contribute to the overall vision. Using the Plan–Do–Check–Act cycle, they then planned what they want to do and constructed some prototypes of what they want to have happen. On several of the projects, they're checking to see if what they designed and tested is working as predicted. This partnership is well on its way to having its vision become a reality—a vision with the potential of saving thousands of lives while improving automobile efficiency and reducing pollution. Partnerships not only add value to business but make dreams come true.

When you're doing strategic planning within a partnership, your partner must be present to engage in the activity. Once you've committed to partnership, you must invite that partner into the planning process with you. KLM and Northwest Airlines do joint strategic planning for the marketing of the flight schedules. Coca-Cola and McDonald's launch promotional activities as a result of strategic planning. To get additional value from the partnership, the partners must engage in some strategic thinking and thus planning in order to achieve the outcome they both desire.

The outline presented here is a format I've used to help partners get the greatest value from their partnership. Based on the Holistic Organization Model (Figure 5 in Chapter 4), it explores both the ethereal and material realms of each business. With this format you can see how these two separate entities will complement and support

Chart 6

Partners' Vision Statement

Vision Statement of Partner 1	Vision Statement of Partner 2
To enhance the value of our investors' portfolios through long-term investing strategies while building trust and confidence by using the most rigorous financial analysis tools and face-to-face research to ensure investment security	To provide our customers with the highest level of banking products and services with convenience and a safe and friendly attitude

each other as they create the outcome: the product or service they want to deliver. Starting at the top of the model I ask the partners to explain their organization's vision. Chart 6 presents an example of two visions—one from a well-known bank and the other from an investment firm. These two businesses were planning to undertake a joint marketing program to the bank's customers in order to expand investment opportunities and generate new customers for the bank.

On the surface, the vision statements in Chart 6 complement each other. The question that partners should ask themselves while strategically planning their partnership is this: "Based on these vision statements, what are the commonalities and the differences?" Then they can brainstorm the commonalities and differences and list them on a flipchart for everyone to review. Is there some difference that would prevent the two organizations from creating a joint marketing plan?

The next items I investigated were the organizational values and ethics. Since both firms are financial in nature, I had each group brainstorm its values and ethics and then review them for compatibility (Chart 7). Based on the two lists, there seemed to be no serious gaps in the two partners' values and ethics. There was, however, some discussion about the value of community involvement and the investment firm's apparent lack of interest in it.

The next area I investigated was the organizations' cultural environment. The Cultural Assessment Grid (Chart 8) was created to guide the discussion between the two partners and yield greater insight into the issues that might arise because of differences in culture. Based

Chart 7

Partnership Values and Ethics List

Values/Ethics: Partner 1	Values/Ethics: Partner 2
• Integrity • Trust • Client confidentiality • Honesty • Rigorous analysis • Loyalty to client	• Security • Safety • Trust • Client confidentiality • Honesty • Friendliness • Community involvement

Chart 8

Cultural Assessment Grid

Cultural Environment	Partner 1	Partner 2
Organizational morale	High	Leadership: High Employees: Medium
Understanding of mission	High	High
Level of stress	High	Low
Level of acceptable risk	High	Low
Win-win orientation	Win-win	Competitive
Ability to trust	Medium	Medium
Past/future orientation	Future	Past
Comfort with change	High	Very low
Comfort with interdependence	Highly independent	Interdependent
Self-disclosure and feedback	Low	Medium

on this information, the partners decided that before they launched any joint marketing initiatives, they needed to do some work within the cultures of the two organizations. While the investment managers were comfortable with change, for example, the banking managers would have trouble integrating the new investment products and services into their daily work. The group decided to help by providing extensive course offerings to help increase the comfort level with these products.

Now that the partners understood the ethereal qualities of the businesses, the next area of discussion concerned the material aspects. The first area we reviewed was differences that would help or hinder the partnership from an organizational structure perspective. Again I used a matrix to help guide the discussion and enable the partners to view their organizations from a holistic perspective. (See Exercise 8.) Next to each category the partners described the structure or issues pertaining to that component of the organization.

The last piece of information the partners needed to discuss before they could begin a formal strategic planning session was the external impacts on the partnership. In Exercise 9, the matrix lists the issues that partners will want to explore to ensure they've covered all the potential traps that might derail the partnership—before they spend time, money, and energy creating a strategic plan. Each partner describes the current status of the external influence.

TIME TO START PLANNING

You are now equipped to begin your strategic planning. You'll also need to use the information you gathered from your internal assessment in Chapter 4. Probably the most valuable information you'll need at this point is your Organizational Process Model (Figure 7) because this will help you and your partner determine how to integrate the two organization processes to provide the value-added component your partnership was created for.

Sharing Information and Resources

Now that you've built a level of trust through your joint strategic planning, you can begin to share information and resources with each other. I know of a french-fry producer who liked the potatoes of a certain farmer in Idaho. Unfortunately, the potato farmer could not produce the

Exercise 8. Organizational Structure Matrix		
Organizational Structure	**Partner 1**	**Partner 2**
Organizational hierarchy		
Reporting relationships		
Communication patterns		
Decision-making strategies		
Reward structure		
Marketing initiatives		
Accountability systems		
Organizational norms		
Legal and regulatory issues		
R&D issues		
Informational technologies		

number of potatoes required by the producer because he didn't have enough acreage. So the producer bought a nearby parcel of land and gave it to the farmer to use, and over a ten-year contract the land became the farmer's property. Both sides benefited: The farmer received a fair price for the potatoes he produced on the land; the producer increased his supply of potatoes. Partners who invest in each other's success both achieve more.

Here's another example of partners investing in each other's success. I know of a company that paid to have consultants teach strategic

Exercise 9. External Impacts on the Partnership		
External Issue	**Partner 1**	**Partner 2**
Board of directors/owners/ stockholders		
Clients/customers		
Government regulatory agencies/ accrediting organizations		
Suppliers		
Unions/employee groups/ professional associations		
Political groups		
Communities		
Competing organizations		

planning to their employees' union. Many members of management were dumbfounded when they heard about this. They wondered why the company would pay to have the union become more organized and stronger through company-provided strategic planning. When the question was asked of the CEO, her answer demonstrated her high PQ: "In the next round of negotiations with the union, I want them to know what their members want so we can get down to the critical issues that are facing our industry. Neither side wants to drag out these talks. It's an investment in our management's time to have the union be strategically prepared for these negotiations."

Sharing Success

A new dynamic occurs when organizations make the paradigm shift from "me" to "we." This is when they move from independence to interdependence. When an organization has increased its PQ enough to understand that its success depends on the partnership's success, it integrates the partnership into the culture. It is now the way "things are done around here."

The more skilled the partnership is in using PQ attributes, the better is the relationship between members. As we shall see in Part Two, these attributes are portable—that is, you can use them in many different settings. When employees learn to improve their PQ on the job, they'll use these skills not only between themselves but when working with customers and even in their personal lives. Employees show higher morale and cultivate better relationships when they communicate effectively. These elements lead to increased productivity. Since business relies on relationships, customers will continue to support organizations with which they've built a good relationship. The organization wins in many ways.

Achieving Full Partnership

Full partnership is not the end of the road. As we develop more trust with our partners, as we achieve predetermined worthwhile goals, as our desire to benefit personally from the arrangement is sustained, our commitment deepens. As in the stages of relationship development, partnerships can revert to earlier stages—back to reassessing needs and redefining what we want from our partners. Just as we reestablish a norming stage following a return to storming, we can recommit to a partnership that we have chosen to redirect. In both cases, the establishment of trust sustains the partners through setbacks and potential turmoil.

Our commitment to a full partnership, therefore, is not a final destination but an ongoing process. The relationships are performing, the synergies are generating mutual benefits, and the partnership is established. *Sustaining* its growth is the challenge. At this point we may want to do some strategic planning. This planning can be done within the boundaries of the partnership to create a mutual future, or it can be done in a larger arena. Many companies present organizationwide "future search" conferences where they invite their partners and try to envision what their partnerships will look like five or ten or twenty years down the road. The more mutual the planning, the deeper the relationship. Trust is a catalyst propelling people into the creative zone.

When partners have reached full partnership, remarkable things start to happen. While the road is tricky and fraught with peril, the rewards can be rich. Full partnerships between organizations are the equivalent of Olympic gold. Many try, few succeed. But those who do succeed know the work involved and the skill it takes to be the best. Here are some of the rewards that full partnerships bring to organizations:

High trust enables creative risk. Only when we trust each other can we risk the quantum leap into the next generation of activity. Regardless of service or products, to move beyond the status quo takes a special talent—and that talent is best tapped into through partnerships. Some of the best breakthough examples come from the American effort to conquer space. The partnerships developed between NASA and private industry are too numerous to list. Certainly more than the drink called Tang came from these partnerships. From microwave ovens to insulated clothing, our lives have changed dramatically. The creative risk taking was there. And those who formed partnerships with NASA stood to benefit like no other.

Open systems increase information and intelligence. The more we share information, the more we learn. Different people can draw different conclusions from the same information and so it's invaluable. Information is the best example of abundance. There's no limit on the amount and how it can be used. Consequently, the more we have and use, the more beneficial it becomes. Organizations that have established trust and full partnership will benefit from this abundance of information and increased intelligence.

Mutual benefits = more for everyone. Again, the theory of abundance becomes reality in this dynamic. The more people benefit from an activity, the more they are willing to engage in it and the more it brings them. It is through partnerships that mutual benefits can be realized, generating wealth for everyone involved.

Partnerships provide value that competitors cannot duplicate. Anyone can reproduce a widget. So don't bet the family fortune on your product or service. Sooner or later, someone will dissect it, figure it out, and make it better. And where will that leave you? What they can never reproduce is the dynamics created through partnerships. Each partnership is unique, made up of unique individuals, and the interactions between these people cannot be replicated. How do you reproduce genius? If scientists could figure out that one, cloning would be the most prevalent form of reproduction. But we haven't figured it out because it is so complex and is the sum of so many factors that it can never be duplicated. This is true of partnerships as well.

Win-win orientation = synergy. Organizations that increase their PQ already know how to create win-win conflict resolution and problem solving. This ability drives fear out of the relationship, lets creativity emerge, and generates the pure gold of partnership: synergy. But synergy is the outcome of a combination of components—the basic skills of partnering intelligence. You cannot have just one or two of these components. All must be there or the partnership will not generate the synergy to move into the creative zone and blast itself away from the competition.

Continuous improvement as well as reshaping strategies and processes as missions and values change are ongoing mandates. All living entities redefine themselves daily by what they do and the environment they live in. Full partnership is not the end of the cycle, but it does represent the ideal culture in which we work. We must dedicate ourselves to making our partnerships as full as they can be every day. If we are accountable for ourselves—and are intelligent enough to work with others in partnership—we will achieve our brightest futures! You will succeed.

COMMITTING STAGE
PLAN–DO–CHECK–ACT CYCLE

You've initiated an activity. Was it successful? Did you need to go back and refine the plan? Was it a bomb? What measurements and indicators did you establish to measure its success? How did the relationship develop? Were there trust and mutual benefits for all the partners? Are you ready to move to the next step? You want to tap into the synergistic energies this partnership has brought you. Are you ready to incorporate the partnership into your strategic planning process? Review the steps and tools in Chapter 7 for the Committing Stage. You can build quality into the process by using the Plan–Do–Check–Act cycle of continuous improvement. This can be accomplished by listing the tasks that need to occur in the Committing Stage below each step of the Plan–Do–Check–Act cycle. On the following pages, I have put together a sample of what to do in each step. You may want to use this example as is or modify it to meet your particular objectives. Either way, it will help you accomplish the task in less time and with greater efficiency and higher quality.

PLAN

At this stage in the partnership, you and your partner have already completed an initial activity together. You've had an opportunity to evaluate the activity and give each other feedback. You are now ready to determine whether the partnership is right for both of you. Review the items listed here:

- Formal commitment to partnership
- Mutual strategic planning
- Sharing of information and resources
- Organizational ownership

The first thing is to formalize your commitment. Then you'll need to decide which items should be addressed as the partnership matures.

DO

Conduct a joint partnership meeting to address these issues. Decide how you want to address the strategic planning. In some organizations, the partners do their own strategic planning. In others, they integrate their strategic planning within the organization's strategic plan. Thus if "Partnering with Our Employees" is an overall organizational goal, then the employees and managers develop a strategic and tactical plan to accomplish it. If you're partnering with another organization but only your marketing departments are involved, you might do the strategic planning just between the two marketing departments. A more straightforward type of strategic planning would occur between a manufacturer and its suppliers. They might plan a year in advance for the levels of activity, the timing of the activity, and any design modifications that should be communicated.

CHECK

How well did the meeting go? Did you meet all the partner's expectations? What would you do better next time? Did you list all the "pluses and deltas" to determine what could be done better next time?

ACT

Are you in full partnership? If not, where do you go from here? At this point, you are back in the planning portion of the Plan–Do–Check–Act cycle.

INTERNAL PARTNERSHIP: CONVENTION HOTEL

Jean and Marty were so pleased with the outcome of their initial activity together that they decided to expand this concept. Beyond making sure that maintenance and housekeeping didn't hinder each other's work, they brainstormed a list of other activities where they might work together. Some of the ideas they came up with included ways that maintenance could help the housekeepers move heavy objects, discussions about the installation of low-maintenance bathroom accessories, and helping in the laundry services. Maintenance came up with a method of attaching various housekeeping implements to the housekeeper's service cart that would require less lifting and reduce back strains. The two departments began to work together so well that Eric, the hotel's general manager, started a partnership between sales and catering. But that is a different story.

EXTERNAL PARTNERSHIP: DOWNTOWN OFFICE TOWER

For John and Peter, their partnership continued through the project until the completion of the building. Because of the relationship established between the Building and Construction Trades Council and the contractor, there were no issues that could not be resolved. And since there was a no-strike clause in their agreement, the building was completed ahead of schedule. In fact, the project was finished two months ahead of the promised date and came in several million dollars under budget.

The law firm was pleased; the contractor was pleased; and, perhaps surprisingly, the unions were pleased. Although their members finished two months early, they did not lose any work. Why? Because the Project Partnering Agreement has worked so well on construction projects that more and more contractors are insisting on having them in place—and that ensures the continual use of union labor. Members of the union construction and building trades have secure jobs for years to come. Thus everyone won. This partnership not only created value for the organizations but has created strategic alliances between building contractors and unions to the benefit of all.

PART THREE

Developing Your PQ

Enhancing Your Partnering Skills

We've covered a lot of material. You now understand the importance of partnerships and how they can add value to your business. You've gotten the concept of PQ—the measure of partnering intelligence—and you've taken the PQ Assessment (Survey 1) to help you determine your personal level of partnering intelligence. You've learned about the Partnership Continuum—the process to follow for creating highly successful, mutually beneficial, and trustworthy partnerships. You understand the three components that make up the Partnership Continuum:

- Stages of relationship development

- Stages of partnership development

- Past/future orientation environment

Moreover, you now understand the need to have balance between the task and relationship aspects of the partnership. You've followed the stages of partnership development. You've assessed your needs. You've searched for the perfect partner. You've discovered a partner with whom you can attain mutual benefits. You committed to participate in an initial activity, and then you evaluated that activity to determine whether the task and relationship dynamics were healthy and productive for both of you. Finally, you committed to full partnership. You jointly created a strategic plan to ensure your mutual success. You saw the partnership move from a past orientation to a future orientation based on trust and commitment.

You've gone through the stages of relationship development, too. First there was the forming stage and people were polite. Then came the storming stage and partners began to assert their needs. But you managed to create win-win solutions and moved to establishing partnership norms. You went on to achieve the highly creative and productive performing stage and lived happily ever after, right?

Sometimes partnerships aren't that easy. In fact, they are rarely that easy. The preceding scenario happens only in an ideal world with perfect human beings. But human beings aren't perfect. I confess I've made many mistakes in my partnering efforts. But I understand that if I want a good partnership, I need to be a good partner. Even the best blueprint for partnering—such as the Partnership Continuum—cannot make up for a low PQ. The model works only as well as the people who are using it. And while using a blueprint is better than just letting your partnership evolve through happenstance, it is the individuals in the partnership who must have the skills to make it work.

Now that you know your PQ, you may be asking how you can improve it. To increase your PQ, you need to know how to use the six basic partnering attributes:

- Past/future orientation in decision making

- Comfort with change

- Win-win orientation in conflict resolution and problem solving

- Comfort with interdependence

- Ability to trust

- Self-disclosure and feedback

In Part Three we'll examine these six attributes. You can start by going back to Chapter 2 and reviewing your ranking on the PQ Assessment (Survey 1). Then go right to Chapter 8 and analyze your PQ using the Attribute Analysis (Survey 3). This tool will point to your strengths and indicate areas for improvement. Once you're familiar with this material, share it with your partners, your friends, and even your family. It's important information that can improve the quality of your life.

A business that invests in developing the six PQ attributes will start to see exciting outcomes. Because these are second-level change processes—that is, they focus on the individual rather than on the world around us—the impact is more immediate and longer lasting. Companies that invest in developing them will experience less internal conflict, more productivity, more creativity, and higher morale than companies that don't. As we shall see in the following chapters, these are the tools that create trust between people and aid in equalizing power. Regardless of our rank, if we can begin to communicate like equals we can begin to act like equals. Without trust and a sense of balance, there can be no productive partnership. Regardless of its desire for strong external relationships, a company that lacks internal PQ will have problems with its partners.

In the next eight chapters, we'll cover all six attributes for increasing your partnering intelligence. In Chapter 8, we start off by analyzing your PQ using the Attribute Analysis. The next six chapters describe each of the six attributes and provide you with self-assessments to help you determine your own ability. I'll also provide techniques to help you use these invaluable tools for improving your PQ. In Chapter 15, we come full circle and I describe some of the hallmarks of great partnerships.

Each of the next eight chapters offers you insights and techniques for improving your partnering intelligence. Start with the areas in which you need the most improvement and then go back to the ones in which you're already competent. A little refresher course never hurt anyone. But above all, enjoy learning more about yourself as you learn to become a great partner.

CHAPTER EIGHT

Analyzing Your Results on the PQ Assessment

Using the Attribute Analysis

Now that you've assessed your relative PQ—your partnering quotient—you may want to determine your strengths and weaknesses in terms of forming a partnership. This information can be used as a predictive tool to raise your awareness and prevent you from neglecting aspects of the partnership that will cause you problems later on. Or it can be used as a diagnostic tool to help you determine why your partnership isn't working as well as you had hoped.

ASSESSING YOUR STRENGTHS

To assist you in determining where you stand in relation to the attributes measured on the PQ Assessment (Survey 1), you can use the Attribute Analysis (Survey 3). This tool aligns the thirty statements with the specific attributes they support. This allows you to determine whether you rank high, medium, or low in the attributes. By completing Survey 3 and its interpretation grid, you will gain new insight into the strengths you bring to a partnership. You can also predict trouble spots where you may want to take some preventive action.

Survey 3
Attribute Analysis

Instructions

On the left-hand side of this survey are the six attributes measured in the PQ Assessment (Survey 1). Beneath each attribute are the numbers of the statements that support this attribute. Go back to the PQ Assessment and find your rank for each statement. Record your rank for each statement in the appropriate space on Survey 3. Then total the score for each attribute. Calculate the average based on the formula beneath each list of statements. On the right-hand side of the survey is a scale showing the lowest and highest possible number for each attribute. Circle the average score for each attribute on the scale. This will indicate whether you ranked high, medium, or low in that attribute.

Example

Low ⟶ Medium ⟶ High

Circle One

Past/Future Orientation

1   2   ③   4   5   6

Statement 1: __4__
Statement 11: __1__
Statement 17: __3__
Statement 19: __4__
Statement 25: __2__

Total Score: __14__
Divide by 5 = __2.8__

Attribute Analysis

Low ⟶ Medium ⟶ High

Circle One

1. Past/Future Orientation

1   2   3   4   5   6

Statement 1: ___
Statement 11: ___
Statement 17: ___
Statement 19: ___
Statement 25: ___

Total Score: ___
Divide by 5 = ___

Attribute Analysis *continued*	Low ➝ Medium ➝ High
	Circle One

2. Comfort with Change

1 2 3 4 5 6

Statement 2: ___
Statement 5: ___
Statement 12: ___
Statement 18: ___
Statement 27: ___

Total Score: ___
Divide by 5 = ___

3. Win-Win Orientation

1 2 3 4 5 6

Statement 3: ___
Statement 13: ___
Statement 20: ___
Statement 23: ___
Statement 30: ___

Total Score: ___
Divide by 5 = ___

4. Comfort with Interdependence

1 2 3 4 5 6

Statement 4: ___
Statement 6: ___
Statement 10: ___
Statement 14: ___
Statement 29: ___

Total Score: ___
Divide by 5 = ___

5. Ability to Trust

1 2 3 4 5 6

Statement 7: ___
Statement 9: ___
Statement 15: ___
Statement 22: ___
Statement 26: ___

Total Score: ___
Divide by 5 = ___

6. Self-Disclosure and Feedback

1 2 3 4 5 6

Statement 8: ___
Statement 16: ___
Statement 21: ___
Statement 24: ___
Statement 28: ___

Total Score: ___
Divide by 5 = ___

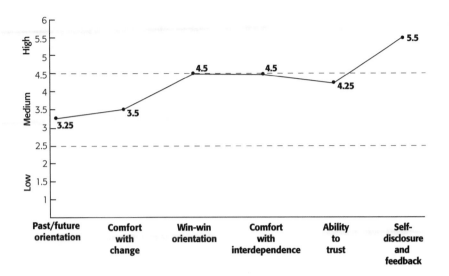

Interpretation Grid for Attribute Analysis

Scoring

Now that you have completed the Attribute Analysis, you'll want to know what it means. Each of the six attributes contributed to your overall partnering intelligence. Most of us have strengths in some attributes and weaknesses in others. Since partnering intelligence requires you to be capable in all six attributes, you'll want to know which ones you are low and high in. The interpretation grid (above) is designed to give you an overall picture of your current level of competence in all six attributes. It shows how you scored in each of the separate attributes and helps you see where you need to improve.

Starting with the first attribute (Past/future orientation), note your average score. If your average score was 3.25, for example, then make a mark on the first vertical line at the 3.25 point on the vertical scale. Continue this procedure across the bottom of the grid until you've completed all six attributes. Once you have scored all six attributes, connect the six points with a line. This is your overall ranking of how you scored on each of the attributes. Note that the vertical axis is divided into three sections: low, medium, and high. These sections correspond to the interpretation grid you completed for the Attribute Analysis.

INTERPRETING THE RESULTS

By now you may be thinking: "Fine, this is great information. But what does it mean and how does it contribute to improving my PQ?" Each attribute is an important skill you'll need in order to succeed on the Partnership Continuum. Because partnerships are systems composed of essential components, if you're lacking in just one skill the system cannot work properly.

Past/Future Orientation

If you scored low in this attribute, it means that you tend to rely on past history when making decisions about future events. If you scored high, you tend to use a planning style and then hold people accountable for doing what they say they'll do. This is a future orientation. If you have a *past* orientation, there tends to be low trust—since you probably don't trust people to do anything other than what they've done in the past. This assumption stifles any hope that things might be different and thus reduces the possibility for change. The outcome of this dynamic is a past orientation and a preference for the status quo. The outcome of a future orientation is a step toward building trust between people. People who scored low in this attribute should pay special attention to Chapter 9.

Comfort with Change

If you scored low in this attribute, it probably means that you're uneasy about change. You like to do things the way they've always been done in the past and are uncomfortable with trying new things. If you ranked high, you probably like change—and may even embrace it. And if you are comfortable with change, you probably also have a future orientation in your decision-making style and a high ability to trust. People who are uncomfortable with change tend to stick to the status quo, have a low ability to trust, and may rely on a past orientation to make decisions. People who scored low in this attribute will want to pay special attention to Chapter 10.

Win-Win Orientation

If you scored low in this attribute, you probably use a win-lose style of problem solving and conflict resolution. This is especially true if you are a competitive person. Competitive conflict resolution and problem-solving techniques, by their very nature, are designed to help one side meet its needs. In a partnership, this is destructive behavior. If you scored high in

this attribute, you are more likely to use a win-win style for conflict resolution and problem solving. People with this style generally have a
higher ability to trust and feel more comfortable being interdependent with others. People who scored low in this attribute will want to
pay special attention to Chapter 11.

Comfort with Interdependence

If you scored low in this attribute, you probably tend to be a highly independent person. While this is a valuable trait in many cases, it can be
destructive in a partnership. Have you ever worked on a project and had
someone go off on a tangent, leaving the rest of the team lost and bewil-
dered? Genius, of course, often requires independent thinking. But in
partnerships, success comes from planning with others and then performing according to plan. If you're uncomfortable relying on others for
your success, you'll have a difficult time being in partnership with others.
People who are strongly independent also tend to have a low ability to
trust, feel discomfort with self-disclosure and feedback, and may be
uncomfortable with change they cannot exclusively control. If you
ranked high in this attribute, you probably are comfortable being interdependent and working in partnership. You may also have a high ability
to trust and comfort with self-disclosure and feedback. If you scored low,
you'll want to pay special attention to Chapter 12.

Ability to Trust

If you scored low in this attribute, you tend to have a low ability to trust
that people will do what they promise. Certain people do condition us
to expect the worst of them. But when we get caught up in that kind of
thinking, a series of cascading events can actually set up the expected
disappointment. People who have a low ability to trust also tend to
have a high need for independence, rely on a past orientation in their
decision-making style, and use a win-lose style of conflict resolution
and problem solving. If you scored high in this attribute, you generally
trust that people will do what they say. In turn you may tend to use a
future-oriented decision-making style, may be comfortable with interdependence, and may be predisposed to use a win-win style of conflict

resolution and problem solving. If you scored low, you may want to pay special attention to Chapter 13.

Self-Disclosure and Feedback

If you scored low in this attribute, you may want to review your level of comfort with disclosing information about yourself. In a partnership, you must be able to express your needs to your partner. An inability to articulate what you need from the partnership will ultimately cause resentment and anger when over time you see your partner getting everything he or she wants while your needs go unmet. The outcome is passive/aggressive behavior—a sure killer of partnerships. Once this pattern is introduced into the partnership, trust is eroded, win-lose conflict and problem solving resolution predominates, and independent behavior takes over as people struggle to salvage what's left of a dysfunctional partnership. In a partnership, you must be able to ask for what you need. This is why we spend so much time in the Partnership Continuum doing a needs assessment. And once you know what you need, you have to feel confident asking for it. Your ability to self-disclose also sends a coded message to partners about your willingness to share. If everyone is talking about his or her personal life but you never confide anything, what do you think the reaction is going to be? If you scored high in this attribute, you're probably able to ask for what you need. This ability tends to build trust between people—at least they know where you stand. You're probably comfortable with interdependence as well, since you know your needs will not be left out of the equation. And you're probably comfortable using a win-win stye of conflict resolution and problem solving since you're confident your needs will be addressed. If you scored low in this attribute, you'll want to pay special attention to Chapter 14.

DEBRIEFING

Now that you've taken the PQ Assessment (Survey 1) and the Attribute Analysis (Survey 3), you'll want to understand what this means to you. Spend some time thinking about the feedback these tools have yielded and reflect on what the information means to you.

Questions to Think About

Review the PQ Assessment (Survey 1):

- Does the score seem to fit with your experience?
- Does it reflect how you feel about your business partnerships?
- What about your personal partnerships?
- If the score seems low, why do you think this is so?

Then review the Attribute Analysis (Survey 3):

- Is there anything here that surprises you?
- Did your scores reflect what you thought they might?
- What does this tell you about yourself?
- What insights has this provided regarding your current partnerships?
- Are the areas in which you scored low trouble spots for you? If so, what is the next step?

Develop an Action Plan

One of the first things you'll want to do after completing the PQ Assessment and the Attribute Analysis is decide if there are areas for improvement. If you scored low in any of the partnering attributes, try using the exercises and skills in this part of the book. The main components of your action plan should address these basic questions:

- Why do I need to do something?
- What do I need to do?
- When do I need to get it done by?
- Who needs to be involved?
- How will I accomplish it?
- Where am I going to do it?

While these questions may not all be appropriate, think about your personal action plan to improve your partnering quotient. And remember: Unlike your IQ, you can increase your PQ.

CHAPTER NINE

Past/Future Orientation in Decision Making

Escaping the Trap of the Past

What happens when you open yourself up to future possibilities? This is what the concept of future orientation decision making is all about. Here we explore the ability to recognize—even welcome—the potential, the unexpected, the new.

Whether an organization is closed or open to new information is determined by whether it has a past or future orientation. Past orientation is associated with a closed paradigm. By this I mean that we make decisions on the basis of past information and reject or ignore new information. The traits we observe in a past orientation include:

- Reliance on past history for decision making
- Independent relationships
- Strong need for control
- Need to maintain the status quo
- Low trust
- Win-lose conflict resolution style

Those operating in a closed paradigm view the world the way they *want* it to be. They're unwilling to challenge their own assumptions and change their beliefs. They make decisions based on outdated mental maps. They are living in the past with old information.

Let me illustrate the power of a closed paradigm. I once worked with the director of a telephone company to establish a self-managed group of technicians responsible for telephone service repair in a western state. The managers who reported to the director were initially reluctant to try a self-managed group because they thought their employees were lazy and would take advantage of a self-managing environment. But a nine-month trial demonstrated that the self-managed team was more productive and did higher-quality work than the traditional work team with a supervisor. In fact, the self-managed team completed a greater number of repair calls and had a lower rate of repeat visits. With these impressive results, I expected the organization to embrace the new method and expand its use.

I was wrong. Despite documented evidence of the self-managed team's success, the managers clung to their old perception. Moreover, their stubbornness proved to be a powerful influence on the director, who dismantled the self-managed team. The data regarding the team's performance were kept from the rest of the organization simply because the managers refused to update their beliefs or disturb the status quo. They still believed the employees needed supervision or they would not work. When reality contradicted their beliefs, they preferred to suppress the data rather than change their mental maps.

MENTAL MAPS: THE MAGIC AND THE TRAP

To make partnerships work, there must be a shift in orientation from past to future. Past orientation, just like past experience, is helpful to the partnership only to the extent that the past can teach us how to accomplish new tasks. When learning something new, you don't want to throw out the baby with the bathwater. History teaches valuable lessons and it's important to remember them. Too often, however, people cling desperately to their experience and fail to move beyond even the forming stage of relationship development. They refuse to give up the old. And yet they cannot embrace the new. This is because of a very powerful human survival technique known as *knowledge transference*—or what I call mental maps.

Here's how mental maps work. Whenever we engage in a new relationship, the first thing we do is scan our personal data bank—our memory—for what we already know about the other person or group.

From our memory we seek out past experiences we've had with them or people like them. A mental scan then produces a map that helps us decide how we want to approach this new experience. Thus we base our decision on the recollected memory of what has happened to us in the past. This knowledge transference occurs whenever we transfer an opinion about one type of person or group to another.

By using this practical cognitive technique, human beings have learned about life and survived on their own even in new and unfamiliar situations. A primitive example of this knowledge transference is the lesson most of us learned at a very young age about fire. We were told not to touch it because it was hot. Fire hurts! Most of us heeded that advice. Furthermore, if we happened to get burned inadvertently, the accident did something very important for us. It reinforced our knowledge that fire is hot and it will burn and hurt if we touch it. Since we don't enjoy pain, we created a mental map about fire and avoided touching it. Now, as adults, we make decisions about fire based on our past orientation.

To demonstrate how we use mental maps I've created a flowchart (Figure 8). While the human decision-making process includes an incalculable number of variables, this simple model shows how we continue to create new mental maps and reinforce old ones. First something happens to us. We experience a new event (box 1). The first thing we do is instantaneously scan our memory (box 2) to see if we've had any similar experiences. Generally at an unconscious level, we ask (box 3): Have I had an experience like this? In most cases, especially as we get older and have more life experiences behind us, we'll identify some experience that resembles the current situation. Our mind scans for a similar pattern. If it finds one, we move on to the next decision. We try to remember the outcome: Was it successful for us (box 4)? This is an internal value judgment. We make this judgment based on our psychology and personality at that moment in our life. Most likely we judge "success" by whether the outcome got us what we needed. If we judge the previous outcome to have been successful, we'll duplicate the behavior (box 5) to match our mental map and will expect a similar outcome. The aftermath of the experience reinforces our mental map (box 6) as the "right" reaction to that experience.

If we've never had an experience like this before (box 3) we'll have to determine our behavior (box 7). The aftermath of that behavior will

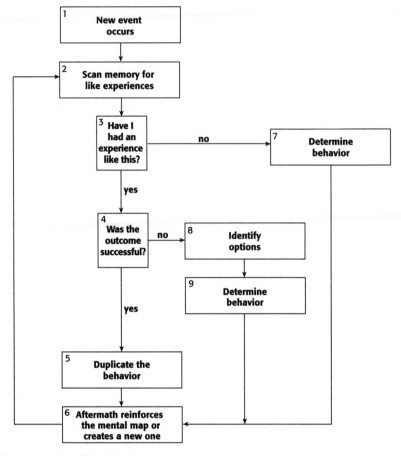

Figure 8   Mental Map Matrix

then create a new mental map for us (box 6) and store it for future use. If we determine our last outcome was unsuccessful (box 4), we'll identify what options we have (box 8). Based on these options, we'll determine a new behavior (box 9), and the aftermath will then create a new mental map for us (box 6) based on the new behavior. The new behavior will be stored in our memory until we need to draw on that experience again. While this process may look complicated on a flowchart, it works instantaneously in our mind and we make snap decisions based on our ability to use knowledge transference.

In relationships we use a similar dynamic. On a social level, we generalize our knowledge to encompass whole groups of people who may look or act alike, although they may not match our mental map exactly. This is the basis for the concept of stereotyping. Based on our interaction with one or two people who belong to that profession, for example, we may lump all engineers, doctors, or lawyers into the same mental map. Or, because we know how to drive a Ford, we may think we know how to drive a Chevrolet or a Plymouth, too, since driving another car fits our mental map of driving a Ford.

Our mental maps don't always work, however, either with people or with activities. I own a 1952 Studebaker Champion convertible that I drive as much as I can during the brief Minnesota summers. One gloriously warm evening I took some friends out to dinner in the Studebaker. At the restaurant, I asked the valet attendant if he knew how to start the car. What I knew (and suspected he didn't) was that to start the motor you have to turn on the ignition with the key and then depress the clutch all the way down to engage the starter. The valet was a cocky young man about eighteen years old. Confidently he advised me he had driven all sorts of cars and knew how to start it. "Okay," I said, and went off to have an enjoyable dinner. Afterward, when I was ready to leave, I gave the ticket to the attendant and waited. I waited long enough for him to fetch my Studebaker from the other side of town.

Finally, the young man appeared. "I don't know what the problem is," he said. "I keep turning the key, but the car won't start."

Again I asked him: "Would you like to know how to start the car?"

"Sure," he sheepishly replied. So I explained to him how to start the car, and moments later he drove up to the door, grinning proudly, behind the wheel of my idling automobile.

While our mental maps are useful in helping us apply what we already know, they are not so helpful when it comes to learning something new. We may think we know something based on an experience and transfer that knowledge to a new experience—only to discover that our mental map is outdated and no longer useful. In a new partnership, we have to be careful how we transfer information based on past history. This is especially challenging, though, since knowledge transference is a common reasoning technique.

Here's the magic of mental maps. A client of mine, the owner of a grocery store chain in the Midwest, wanted to form a partnership with several contractors to rebuild a grocery store in a chic section of town. He needed to keep the store open during the rebuilding process.

Much work was done to bring the store managers and contractors together to talk about the customers' shopping experience during the remodeling. They wanted to figure out how they could partner to not only complete the extensive construction job but also keep people coming in during the remodeling.

The reconstruction went off without a hitch. Although shopping was more of a challenge during that period, people continued to shop there—and, remarkably, sales dropped only a few percentage points. Considering the amount of work, this was an incredible feat. After the contractors and managers agreed on how they would work together in partnership to complete the job without spoiling the customers' experience, the managers used the same partnership-building process—the Partnership Continuum—with the store employees. Employees were under particular stress because they were often required to move stock from one side of the store to another and then be able to direct customers to the new location. Since the new location changed almost nightly for more than a month, there was a huge amount of pressure on everyone. Nevertheless, after partnering with the contractors, the store managers were able to transfer the knowledge they learned to the employees. This created a successful situation for everyone: owner, managers, customers, employees, and contractors. The remodeling was successful; customers continued to shop; and the job was completed on time.

Now here's the trap of mental maps: They often include prejudice or bias about something or someone. In an imperfect society, prejudice is part of our programming. You yourself can probably recall a time when you were misunderstood, discounted, or labeled by someone else who had an inaccurate mental map.

The possibilities of partnership synergy make it worth our while to withhold our prejudices. If we can check ourselves, we have more options. We can avoid the trap and anticipate some magic ahead. Most of all, we can look at the glass as being half full, not half empty. We can assume, that is, that others have more to give us than we can supply for ourselves. The good news is this: We can change. We can let go of our old maps and make new ones. This is especially important as we begin to form partnerships. It's important to be open, to share information, and to dispel the myths that make up many of our mental maps. It increases our partnering intelligence.

With one of my clients, I encountered the concept of "collective" mental maps. Collective memories exist in organizations and turn into powerful myths that defy logic and cause trouble. These myths can become so powerful that when enlightened management tries to overcome them, they are run out of town. In this case I was working with the product manager of a phone company who was responsible for introducing a new product—Caller ID—in a western state. Janice believed the best way to introduce the product was to announce the introduction and call for the public's response. The vice president of the organization didn't agree. He wanted to introduce the product as quickly and quietly as possible—without controversy. While Janice disagreed with this philosophy, the company's culture was very powerful. Leadership disliked any publicity. The best strategy for introducing their product, they insisted, was to quietly seek regulatory permission and then advertise through bill inserts. An alliance of battered women's groups, however, did not want the product introduced at all. It wanted safeguards that would allow a woman to make a call without revealing her number. Then a consumer group that monitors regulated industries discovered what the company was doing—and immediately created a coalition of its constituencies to fight the product's introduction. Months of wrangling over this issue delayed the debut of Caller ID and cost millions of dollars in marketing, advertising, and training expenses.

Had the company been open about its plans, it would have recognized the issues up front and worked with these groups to minimize the product's negative impact. But working with old mental maps, the organization wasn't willing to disclose what it needed to—and was unwilling to risk trusting the advocacy groups to become partners in introducing the product. The telephone company ended up supplying a feature, free of charge, that allows subscribers to block their telephone number from being identified. Instead of a number, the product shows "number unavailable." Although the company had the technology to do this from the beginning, it thought the issue was a minor concern and not worth the slight effort required to implement the blocking feature. Ironically, the delay cost the company many millions of dollars—and many community supporters.

Closed behavior is the response of those operating in a past orientation who need to maintain the status quo. The status quo offers a kind of homeostasis within closed minds or closed systems. Change creates an imbalance between what we believe and what we see occurring around us. A common defense mechanism to help us resolve this state of imbalance—or lack of homeostasis—is the denial mechanism. For most of us, it is easier to deny information than to challenge long-held assumptions based on our history. People operating in a closed paradigm are less trusting and less willing to share decision-making processes. They have a strong need for control. And they refuse to share their future plans lest someone might "steal" them. In this age of industrial sabotage and high-level power plays, there might indeed be some justification in such a reaction. But when weighed against the possibilities of an open paradigm or future orientation—the benefits of sharing the wealth and the knowledge—the positives far outweigh any strategic advantage of secrecy. Secrecy seems pointless anyway. Today's organizations have the ability to replicate almost overnight what they see a competitor doing. The advantages of secrecy, therefore, are minimal.

What is the cost of secrecy to the closed organization? The best way to answer this question is to examine the advantages of an open system. Springfield Remanufacturing Company might be a perfect example of how an open paradigm works. In 1993 when the company was International Harvester's engine rebuilding plant, management decided to close the facility. But the general manager, Jack Stack, knew the business could succeed by creating a partnership with the employees. By passing the hat among the employees and borrowing money from a bank, he had enough to buy the firm. He was able to bring Springfield Remanufacturing back from the dead by using an open management system. In 1995 this company generated $104 million in revenue and at least $2.8 million in net profits. It has experienced a growth rate of at least 15 percent each year since 1993. Stack listed these positive components:

- Employee involvement and ownership
- Sharing of rewards and risks
- Invaluable employee input
- Self-managed organization
- Increased worker education
- A rapidly growing business incubator

Contrast the experiences of the open paradigm used by Springfield with the telephone company's closed paradigm. Organizations that share appropriate information, financial data, and the planning process with their workers and customers are proving to be more efficient and creative organizations with higher quality, higher profits, and higher employee morale.

BACK IN THE PAST OR INTO THE FUTURE?

Historians may argue the significance of variables in the great events that have marked humankind's evolution. They may not dispute facts, dates, and who did what. But trying to explain *why* certain people did what they did touches upon psychology, sociology, spirituality, and a host of other social sciences that are far from factual.

Most historians would agree that people are influenced by the world they live in. The environment—the culture in which we work and live—has a good deal to do with how we think and, therefore, what we end up accomplishing. Albert Einstein said: "The theory to which we subscribe will determine what we see." By this he meant that if you're a pessimist by nature, you'll see the glass as half empty. Perhaps if you're a staunch Democrat, you'll swear all Republicans are partisan. So, too, your ability to create partnerships will be influenced by your environment.

Know Yourself First

One of the most important aspects of creating successful partnerships is to know yourself first. It's essential to understand your own weaknesses, biases, and prejudices. Knowing these things does not make you weaker. In fact, it makes you much stronger. Knowing where you are vulnerable enables you to seek out those who can reinforce and strengthen those areas. Keeping your weaknesses hidden from yourself does not ensure that others won't spot them immediately and exploit them readily. When forming a partnership, knowing yourself is invaluable.

Knowing yourself also relates to business. An organization must have a realistic assessment of its own culture, its way of viewing the world. Understanding the organization's strengths and weaknesses is as critical to a business partnership as understanding your personal pluses and minuses is to a personal partnership.

Rating Your Organization

Some organizations develop patterns of thought that enable partnerships to produce the outcomes desired. Others choose to operate with attitudes that preclude any chance of success.

Reflect on your own organization. (See Survey 4.) What is the orientation where you work: past or future? Your position on the past–future spectrum is indicated by specific characteristics.

Survey 4
Past/Future Orientation Inventory

Instructions

On the rating scale that follows each description, place your organization closer to past orientation (1) or future orientation (5) by circling the appropriate number.

Past/Future Orientation

	Past		Circle One		Future

1. *Win-Lose vs. Win-Win Style of Conflict Resolution and Problem Solving:*
   A win-lose conflict resolution style (past orientation) creates losers. Losers are neither happy nor self-satisfied nor proud. They want to get even. A win-win conflict resolution and problem-solving style (future orientation) works toward achieving a mutually agreeable plan. In terms of its conflict resolution style, is your organization closer to a past orientation or a future orientation?

   1   2   3   4   5

2. *Individual Performance vs. Teamwork:*
   A team spirit requires a certain amount of trust between members (future orientation). Without trust and openness, teams cannot perform well. With no appreciable teamwork, an organization won't achieve potential synergies, nor will it encourage creativity and innovation (past orientation). How would you rate your organization's ability to support the concept of teamwork?

   1   2   3   4   5

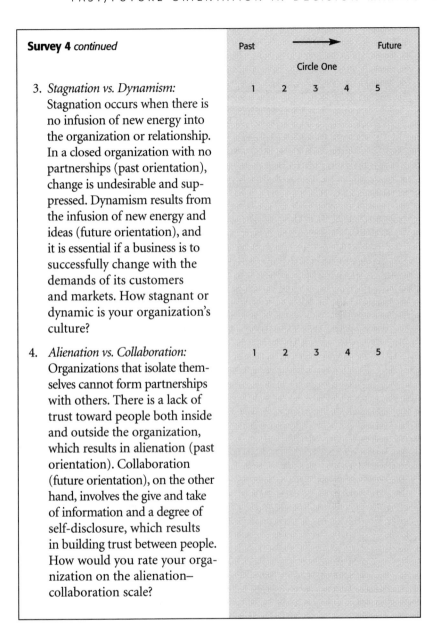

Survey 4 *continued*

Past ⟶ Future

Circle One

3. *Stagnation vs. Dynamism:*
Stagnation occurs when there is
no infusion of new energy into
the organization or relationship.
In a closed organization with no
partnerships (past orientation),
change is undesirable and sup-
pressed. Dynamism results from
the infusion of new energy and
ideas (future orientation), and
it is essential if a business is to
successfully change with the
demands of its customers
and markets. How stagnant or
dynamic is your organization's
culture?

1   2   3   4   5

4. *Alienation vs. Collaboration:*
Organizations that isolate themselves cannot form partnerships
with others. There is a lack of
trust toward people both inside
and outside the organization,
which results in alienation (past
orientation). Collaboration
(future orientation), on the other
hand, involves the give and take
of information and a degree of
self-disclosure, which results
in building trust between people.
How would you rate your organization on the alienation–
collaboration scale?

1   2   3   4   5

Survey 4 *continued*

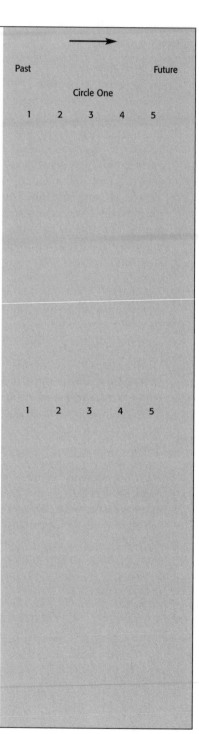

Past   Future

Circle One

5. *High Need for Control vs. Empowering Others:*
In order to form a partnership, we need to release some control over events. If an organization is intent on controlling every aspect of the partnership (past orientation), the partnership will fail. Every partnership must be mutually beneficial; therefore, both partners have to make sure they are benefiting. This does not mean domination of the partnership. Rather, it means empowering others so participants can work collaboratively toward a mutually satisfying result (future orientation). How would you rate your organization on this scale?

1   2   3   4   5

6. *Making Decisions Based on Past Experience vs. Negotiating a Plan and Agreeing on Outcomes*
When organizations continue to make decisions based on past experiences, they limit themselves by not being open to new possibilities (past orientation). Companies wanting to form partnerships need to be willing to negotiate expectations and then hold people accountable for doing what they say they'll do (future orientation). If you continue to hear statements such as "they'll never do that" or "that's not possible," you probably work in an organization that has a past orientation.

1   2   3   4   5

Scoring

For each of the six statements on pages 160–162, fill in your score in the appropriate box in the chart below. A score of 3 or less indicates a weakness in that attribute. You will want to pay particular attention to your weakest attributes as you work to build your partnering intelligence skills.

Statement	Attribute	Points
1	Win-win orientation	
2	Ability to trust	
3	Comfort with change	
4	Self-disclosure and feedback	
5	Comfort with interdependence	
6	Past/future orientation in decision making	

Interpreting the Results

How did your organization rate? The higher the total score, the more you see your organization oriented toward the future. Just as with individual evaluations, the importance of understanding the present reality leads to a decision: Are the people in the organization comfortable where they are? If they are, they won't see a need for change or make any efforts toward that end. What impact might this choice have on future partnerships? And if people do want to change, how can they go about it?

Organizations that want to change their paradigm need to examine themselves. They have to assess their various relationships, both internal and external. Organizations, like other forms of life, experience pain as a warning that something is wrong. It is the people who work in these organizations that manifest the pain. The symptoms include low morale, unethical behavior, isolation, resistance to change, and a feeling of being ignored. Recognizing this pain is the first step in helping an organization begin the change process. This is a necessary step. Before the organization can transform itself from one that does not value collaborating to one that embraces the partnering process, it must acknowledge the problem.

Through openness and a future orientation, an organization can begin to take a realistic look at its culture. By doing this self-analysis, it begins the process of healing the wounds caused by a past orientation. The bad news is that the journey toward openness and a more positive paradigm takes time. The good news is that you can start right now. And you don't have to go through the experience alone. You can use the Partnership Continuum as a guide to increase your partnering intelligence and get you to your destination.

CHAPTER TEN

Comfort with Change

Skills for Coping with Transition

Change is part of our daily lives. Our bodies go through a normal growth and maturity cycle as we change from children to adolescents and then to adults. As our bodies develop, we also mature both mentally and emotionally. Change doesn't end with our bodies and minds. It is a dynamic that affects all of our relationships. And to add to the complexity, people are changing in different ways and at different rates all the time. It's no wonder Heraclitus noted that there is nothing permanent except change.

With all this change occurring around us, it's helpful to remember that while you can't always control change, you can control how you respond to it. Most of us go through three stages when dealing with change: awareness, transition, and new reality.

Sometimes change occurs gradually and sometimes it hits like a lightning bolt. Either way, most of us prefer to ignore it until it reaches our awareness. This is the first of the three stages. When change hits, we feel overwhelmed, shocked, outraged. If we perceive it to be negative or threatening, we may slip back into old behavior to help us cope. We ask ourselves lots of questions: "What's happening?" or "Why is this happening to me?" Even if we perceive the change to be positive, we can be anxious. Remember how it felt when you went to that job interview you were so excited about?

Exercise 10. Partnership Stressors Checklist

Stress Point	Yes	No
1. I am uncomfortable giving up control in a partnership.		
2. I do not feel I can totally trust my partner.		
3. Partnerships feel like too much work.		
4. Partnerships create too much conflict.		
5. Partnerships never get anything accomplished.		
6. Depending on another person creates stress for me.		
7. I dislike having to discuss things about myself.		

Once we acknowledge the change, we begin to feel lost—like we are stumbling in the dark. We know the past is changing, but we're not quite sure what the future looks like. This stage is the transition. During the transition we spend time reflecting on the future, think about what we want, and take action to help move us in that direction. At this point other people help ground us and give us input to gain clarity about our future and the new reality. As the new reality begins to take shape, we feel stronger. This is the third stage. We know more about ourselves and what we want. We're ready to take action and set new goals for ourselves.

Partnerships are a definite source of change. Their very nature ensures that change will occur. Since change is a normal dynamic in a relationship, you'll want to find out what might cause you stress in a partnership. To help you do this, I have created a checklist of the most common stress points in a partnership. Check yes or no in Exercise 10. The items you mark yes indicate areas that may cause you some anxiety when it comes to change. If you dislike giving up control when performing a task, for example, you probably feel stress in a partnership when you have to do a task together. The anxiety you feel is the aftermath of the change you're experiencing. If the stress is negative, you may try to avoid or even deny the change to prevent the anxiety. This is the normal "fight or flight" response we all experience during periods of stress.

If we can't control the change that's occurring around us, at least we can recognize the stressors and develop a plan to deal with them. After you've completed Exercise 10, you'll be in a better position to plan for them. Knowing your stressors and how you react to change is important in helping you cope with change. Understanding is the first step in helping you maintain control of your response to the change.

Partnerships are ripe with stressors. When two people or two organizations come together, things are bound to be different. What sorts of stressors will affect your partnership? Some typical examples might be:

- Team involvement
- Increased risk taking
- Reduced organizational security
- Change of job, type of work, or client
- Feelings about change
- Economic uncertainty and insecurity
- Questions of personal integrity
- Concerns for family, friends, or co-workers

If any of these issues is a stressor for you in forming a partnership, make a list of the objectives you'd like to accomplish for that issue. As you begin to form the partnership, make sure you address these issues with your partner. Develop a plan to ensure that any stressors have a positive outcome.

UNDERSTANDING CHANGE

To help you deal with your partnership stressors, I use a model to explain the dynamic of change (see Figure 9). You can use this model in forming business partnerships as well as in your personal life.

The first step is to know where you're going. You do this by creating a vision of what the change will look like when you've arrived. I once asked a marketing manager to think about what would happen if he partnered with the production manager. He responded by saying: "Well, we'd talk to each other regularly, we'd problem-solve issues, and we'd work together to meet production and shipping deadlines."

Figure 9 Change Model

After thinking about this for a minute, he got very excited and said: "I think I get it! Now all I have to do is put a plan together to accomplish these three items and I'm on my way." "Close," I said. Then I mentioned that it would be helpful if he included his production partner in the discussions. "Oh, yeah," he said, "I forgot about him!" It's easy to forget that it takes two to partner. Yet even the best intentions can go haywire when we forget about the other.

So the first step in creating change is to create a vision of where you want to be. In Figure 9, the future state is the rectangle at the end of the sequence. To achieve something, you first have to know what you *want* to achieve. You need a vision of the future state. You start to think about what the partnership is going to look like, how you will look in the partnership, what the partnership will do. You begin to think about how the partnership will satisfy your needs and those of your partner.

Next assess your current situation. In Figure 9, this is the ellipse at the start of the sequence. What is your current capability? To move to the future state, you must understand what you are currently capable of doing. This requires an internal assessment of your abilities and also your limitations. It's important to assess the current situation accurately so you can see the gap between your current state and the future state.

Once you've assessed the current situation and identified the gap between the current situation and the future state, it's time to develop a transition plan. In Figure 9, this is the arrow. This is your plan for closing the gap between today and tomorrow.

MANAGING CHANGE

Understanding how the change process works is the first step in dealing with change. Now we want to manage the change we're creating. You do this by creating an action plan—even a plan as simple as the one in Chart 9.

Chart 9

Action Plan: Learning to Ride a Bike

What	Who	When	Where
Get a bicycle	Me	Saturday	Midtown Bicycle Shop
Find someone to teach me how to ride it	Neal	Saturday afternoon	High school track
Set aside time to learn to ride it.	Me/Neal	Saturday afternoon	
Find a place to practice	Me		High school track
Find time to practice	Me	After work (Monday, Wednesday, Friday)	High school track

You may be thinking that this action plan is only common sense, and you are absolutely correct. But don't minimize the power of creating a basic plan and then sticking to it. And now that you have a plan, you have taken the first step toward accomplishing your objective. The vision starts to become real when you've made a plan to achieve it. Whether in your personal life or your business life, put the plan down in writing—using this simple format—to establish a framework for when and where things get done. In partnerships success is achieved when things happen. And things happen most efficiently when you have a plan.

Now that you have a plan for dealing with the change, you'll want to implement it. Building a commitment to the change process is the strategy that works best. You've done your homework. You've visualized your future state, assessed your current situation, and developed a plan to move from the current situation to the future state. Now it's time to commit. Chart 10 lists some of the tactics I use in building commitment to change in partnerships.

Chart 10

Building Commitment to Change

- Communicate the vision to your partner (including your needs and expectations).
- Ask for your partner's vision of change (including his or her needs and expectations).
- Allow time to discuss and articulate both visions and needs.
- Ensure that all partners participate in developing the details.
- Leave room for options, choices, and new ideas.
- Share information to minimize any unwelcome surprises.
- Take your time in developing the partnership—don't force an issue.
- Try out new ideas and concepts before making a commitment.
- Demonstrate your commitment to the change that is occurring.
- Avoid creating "winners" and "losers." Be honest—up front and early— about the impacts the change or partnership will have on people.
- Set standards and goals and continue to communicate and provide feedback on outcomes.
- Continue to reward people when they focus on the vision.

MANAGING RESISTANCE

It would, of course, be ideal if people embraced change with zest and unquestionable commitment. But rarely have I worked with partners where that has occurred. Usually I encounter resistance even after we've set up a plan and created an environment in which change can take root. Understanding why people resist change is a big step toward helping them overcome their fear and anxiety. Chart 11 outlines some of the reasons for resistance and offers some remedies to overcome them.

Now that we've gone through some strategies for helping you understand and improve your partnering intelligence as it relates to change, it's time to think about how you manage change in your life and your partnerships. In Exercise 11 (page 172), I want you to recall a change situation that involved a partnership. This partnership— whether personal or business—required you to change how you did something (a task) or how you related to someone (a relationship). At

Chart 11

Common Obstacles to Change

Fear	Remedy
Loss of control	Encourage participation in planning and implementing the partnership.
Uncertainty about the future	Communicate the vision clearly and show how people will fit into the future. Give them the big picture.
Loss of competence	Ensure that people will have the skills to operate in the new partnership.
Loss of familiarity	Create situations in which people can relate to the past while moving into the future. Make links and allow time for transitions.
Surprises	Allow time for people to adjust to new situations and partners. Be honest and share whatever information you have.

the top of the exercise, explain the nature of the change. Then review the six questions. How do these questions relate to the three areas of change highlighted in this section? What issues are related to your change stressors? How can you start to build commitment to change? What issues are related to resistance to change?

BRINGING BALANCE INTO THE PARTNERSHIP

Just as change is a powerful dynamic in the partnership, the ability to balance the change process between the two critical components of partnership—task and relationship—is essential.

No partnership can flourish without this balance. In deference to "getting the job done," it is the relationship component that is most often ignored. But being accountable for our own productivity is only half of the equation. After all, if achieving our goals only required that

Exercise 11. My Change Experience

The change experience was: _____

Question	Events and Feelings I Experienced
1. How did you feel before the change occurred?	
2. What events preceded the change? How did you feel about them?	
3. What was your main concern while the change was occurring?	
4. What was the impact of the change on you? On your partner?	
5. How did you feel after going through the change?	
6. How did you feel about your partner?	

we be accountable for our own actions, we wouldn't need a partner. The other half of the equation is building a trusting relationship with our partner. And this requires us to change not what we might do, but how we do it.

When I work with a group that wants to complete a task but spends no time developing a cooperative relationship, I find their work product to be merely satisfactory. The product meets minimum standards but cannot withstand even minimal changes in requirements. Even slight situational changes mean the group may have to redo the task. Teams that spend all their time on relationship development seem to enjoy the process of working together, but also find they have trouble staying "on task" and finishing the assignment on time. I find their work to be incomplete.

When I see groups spending an equal amount of time on tasks and relationships, I see better outcomes. When a group deliberately moves toward balance, some people who are used to working exclusively on the task or on the relationship may feel awkward. Others in the group can bring them along, however, by acknowledging the

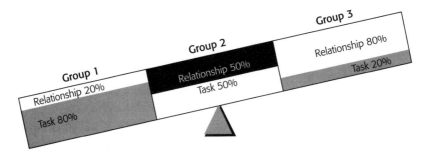

Figure 10   Task/Relationship Model

importance of both kinds of activities. By balancing time and energy between the two activities, people achieve better outcomes. Moreover, they feel better about what they've accomplished together. The group has more pride in what it has produced. The task/relationship model (Figure 10) illustrates the three positions regarding balance.

Group 1: The group meets the requirements of the task, although some partners may feel left out. The "doers" in the group take over and do it. Not everyone in the group feels ownership of the outcome, and not everyone will feel good about the process used in accomplishing the task. A typical comment from a group member: "At least it's done."

Group 2: The group spends its energy developing practical partnerships within the group. They develop relationships *and* work on the task. People complete the task on time, with high quality, and in a creative manner. What contributes to the high functioning of this model is the group's intention to get the job done as a team process. Everyone respects one another and uses everyone's contributions to create the best outcome. A typical comment: "I enjoyed doing the task, I'm proud to have been part of it, and everyone seemed to get along well."

Group 3: The group puts its energy into developing relationships. The "relators" take over and welcome the opportunity to socialize and share information. Although they may not accomplish the entire task in the required time, people feel good about what they do accomplish. At least they develop some short-term relationships. A typical comment: "Even if we didn't finish, I really feel good about what we did."

Do the Task/Relationship Balance Assessment (Exercise 12 on page 174). Have you responded no to any question? If so, answer the following questions to help you pinpoint where the balance is lacking.

Exercise 12. Task/Relationship Balance Assessment		
Question	**Yes**	**No**
1. Is there balance in your relationship with your partner?		
2. Is there balance in the task between you?		
3. Have you talked about the imbalance in your partnership?		

Debriefing Questions

Relationship:

- What leadership issues exist in the partnership that cause the imbalance?
- Does one partner have more control over the relationship? Who?
- Why does one partner have more control?
- Are you equal partners in decision making? If not, why not?
- Do you resolve your conflicts using a win-win style? If not, why not?
- Do you solve problems in a way that benefits all partners? If not, why not?

Task:

- Are you equally engaged in the task? If not, who is doing more or less?
- Is each partner contributing equally to the task in terms of financial support? Time? Energy?
- Are both partners able to provide suggestions and input that is valued and used in completing the task?
- Does the outcome of the task benefit both partners? If not, why not?

Do you notice a trend? Have you been able to isolate where in the task/relationship component there's a lack of balance? What does this tell you about your partnership?

Overall the partnership needs to split its time about 50/50 between the task and relationship aspects of development. This ratio will change, however, as the partnership matures and progresses through the stages of development. Depending on their stage of development, partners shift their energies back and forth between task and relationship. Eventually they'll need to work equally in both areas. When a partnership first forms, for example, partners may spend 80 percent of their time on the relationship and only 20 percent on the task. As they develop more trust, they move toward more tasks together. With maturity, the partnership may be spending 80 percent of its energy on tasks and 20 percent on relationship issues. Knowing where you and your partner stand along this continuum—and knowing in which direction it would be most helpful to move—is critical information to help you be a smarter partner.

The Task/Relationship Model (see Figure 10) is pertinent to the Partnership Continuum because it stresses the balance needed to produce high-quality outcomes. If a partnership focuses only on a task, relationship problems will ultimately emerge and threaten its existence. About four years into the Northwest Airlines–KLM partnership, for instance, John Dasburg, Northwest's CEO, characterized the relationship as "schizophrenic." He was referring to different perceptions of how much each partner controlled the partnership (a relationship issue). Although the partnership had been financially rewarding for both airlines (a task issue), the alliance was in trouble. Regardless of the attractive financial outputs, this question of control threatened to create a divorce case.

In time the two airlines discovered the issues that were preventing them from moving deeper into the relationship. One issue was the number of shares KLM owned in Northwest and the fact that KLM's position gave it a seat on Northwest's board of directors. (Northwest didn't have a representative on KLM's board.)

KLM and Northwest revisited this issue in the interest of improving their partnership. KLM agreed to sell its share in Northwest (and made a significant return on its investment since the shares had appreciated). In exchange, KLM's president resigned from Northwest's board of directors to equalize the power of each partner. As a result, each airline gained more independence—yet a stronger partnership—based on their mutual benefits. Their alliance now is a model of how interdependent entities can create more business for each other. Their relationship creates synergy.

CHAPTER ELEVEN

Win-Win Orientation

From Conflict to Synergy

In industries the world over, partnerships falter and crumble. Organizations large and small strive to work together and create something more than they can create alone—only to have the relationships disintegrate. Remember Quaker and Snapple? Novell and WordPerfect? AT&T and NCR? The confusing aftermath of shattered partnerships usually leaves organizations and employees in turmoil trying to figure out what's next for them. In the process, everyone involved wastes valuable time and resources, not to mention the goodwill of customers, stockholders, suppliers, and employees.

There are two dynamics I look at when I conduct an analysis of broken partnerships: the synergistic opportunities and the styles of conflict resolution. I start with synergy. I want to know about the synergistic possibilities that suggested the partnership in the first place. Partners come together for a reason. Generally, it's the hope of achieving just the right combination of product mix, technology, information, or market access that will differentiate them in the marketplace. They want the golden ring. I want to understand the motivation behind the partnership. What was the vision? Why did these partners come together?

BUSINESSES WANT SYNERGY

It's not news that technology and information are increasing at an exponential growth rate. Many businesses are hard pressed to keep up with the breakneck pace of change. At the same time, people's expectations of products, services, and even relationships are changing. Consumers are more demanding and sophisticated than ever. They want it all. And if they can't get satisfaction from one source, they'll go elsewhere. Businesses and the people running them are struggling to figure out how to meet rising expectations at a time when demands seem to outpace the ability to change.

Whether in our personal life or in business, most of us eventually turn to creating partnerships to help us achieve our goals. Aren't two heads better than one? There's a word that describes the potentially dynamic force created in a partnership: *synergy.* The best definition of synergy I've heard is in the form of a mathematical equation: $1 + 1 > 2$. This is the essence of synergy. It is two (or more) people or organizations working together to do more than one of them can do alone—even after summing up their individual achievements. In nature the concept of synergy is embodied in procreation. One person alone cannot create another human being. Two different people together, however, can create something each could never do separately. The result, a new life, is certainly more than the sum of the parts. Moreover, it is created without taking away from the continued success of each contributor.

Understanding synergy and its potential is indispensable in the formation of partnerships. Do you know what the synergies are in your partnerships? Try answering the following questions:

- What is the synergistic benefit to you in your partnership?
- What is the synergistic benefit to your partner?
- Have you mutually agreed to help each other achieve these benefits?
- How will you measure your achievement?
- How do you tell each other if you're not getting the benefits of the partnership?
- What other opportunities are there to partner within the company? With suppliers? With customers?

While it's important to understand the vision behind the partnership and recognize its synergistic opportunities, they are really just an outcome of the next dynamic: conflict resolution. You cannot have synergy unless you know how to manage conflict. Synergy, in fact, is the outcome of conflict. It happens when conflict is handled in a collaborative, win-win manner.

HARNESSING THE ENERGY OF CONFLICT

Partnerships enable organizations to achieve their vision, and most of the time they look great on paper. But all too often the cultures clash, conflict reigns, and, in the end, everyone loses. While conflict can appear in any part of the Partnership Continuum, it is especially common during the storming stage of relationship development. In the storming stage, conflict erupts and must be resolved. If organizations are in a past orientation and view the conflict competitively, then losers and winners are created. This dooms any hope of synergy moving the partnership into the creative zone.

However attractive a partner may appear, making the partnership work takes time and effort. Companies do not have many problems becoming partners, but they often run into trouble managing their partnerships. The biggest challenges, perhaps, are the partnerships we do not initiate. Sometimes we are forced into partnerships because of the work we do and because today's world is changing so fast. Our bosses, customers, employees, regulators, and even our competitors are changing every day. In the age of instant information, change is the only constant. I've been on the inside with some of the largest conglomerates in America before, during, and after celebrated mergers and takeovers, and I've witnessed both success and bloody dissolution. The human factor is the most powerful variable in the fate of a partnership. How the people who make up these organizations build relationships and accomplish critical tasks invariably determines the outcome of the partnership.

When companies merge, it shakes up the systems of both companies, challenging the old, established paradigms and pouring in new information. Sometimes the new reality feels like a deluge, with the water lapping at our chins. To make the transition successfully, you'll need a high PQ. Did you ever switch to a different school when you were growing up? If you did, you know the anxiety and conflicted feelings people have about developing new partnerships. New partnerships, like new schools, mean new challenges and opportunities, but they also mean conflict.

Conflict is a good thing once you learn to harness the energy it creates. Human beings have only so much energy. If we fritter it away in unproductive conflicts, there's less available to solve problems or be creative. But if we're able to use our energy productively, we can direct it in a way that moves us forward. Conflict presents partners with opportunities to explore the deeply held values they bring to the partnership. It helps them understand each other's position better and forces them to use their communication and feedback skills. It helps establish trust.

Understanding Your Conflict Resolution Style

Everyone has a style of managing conflict. Your conflict resolution style is the mechanism that helps you deal with conflict psychologically. But conflict can create a physical reaction, too. It can cause increased blood pressure and body temperature, for example, which can make a person turn red, perspire, and get nauseated. Conflict can also create psychological stress and trauma—which influence our behavior in a variety of ways from rage, anger, and confrontation (fight responses) to denial, avoidance, and retreat (flight responses). We've created elaborate strategies to cope with conflict in order to maintain control of our situations and get what we want. The challenge is managing conflict in a way that allows each person involved to walk away feeling like a winner. To do this, we must understand the strategies for managing conflict.

According to the classic Thomas-Kilmann model of conflict resolution (*Thomas-Kilmann Conflict Mode Instrument*, 1974), five strategies for managing conflict operate in all cultures:

- *Avoid:* One avoids the other in dealing with conflict or denies that the conflict exists. Avoidance is a lose-lose strategy because neither party has an opportunity to resolve the conflict. Not talking—or physically leaving the scene—means I am unwilling or unable to resolve the conflict.

- *Accommodate:* One gives in to the other at the expense of getting his or her own needs met. Accommodation is a win-lose strategy unless the issue has no importance. Accommodation is a useful goodwill gesture when one party really doesn't care. Letting the other person pay for lunch or enter an elevator first may make that person comfortable and demonstrate your courtesy, but these are not situations of conflict. If I resolve conflicts by accommodating my partner all the time, I'll become resentful and permanently unsatisfied.

- *Compete:* One competes with the other to "win" the conflict. In a competition, one party wins and the other loses. In true competition, there's never a tie. The survival of the fittest creates one winner and many losers—all likely to feel resentful and suspicious of the process. Winning the competition takes precedence over finding a fair solution to the conflict.

- *Compromise:* Each party gives up something he or she needs to achieve a partial solution. This is a lose-lose outcome because both partners give up something of importance. And, ultimately, the partners will address the same issues later. Compromise is useful as a temporary gesture, but it seldom makes either party happy.

- *Collaborate:* Both parties express their needs and resolve the issue to achieve an outcome that allows both sides to get their needs met. While this may sound simple, it is the most difficult strategy to use since it requires that both parties articulate, prioritize, and satisfy their own needs as well as the other's.

Most of us are capable of using all five strategies and, in fact, use a variety of them throughout the day. Our choice of strategy depends on the circumstance, person involved, urgency, importance, and desired outcome. During times of emotional duress, however, we revert to our *primary* strategy for coping with conflict. Psychologists say we are programmed with a primary conflict strategy between birth and approximately three years of age. Regardless of how well trained and educated we are, when we get emotional, even for a brief moment, we revert to this method of resolving conflict.

We generally adopt one of four primary strategies by age three: avoid, accommodate, compete, or compromise. Unfortunately, only collaboration can resolve conflict, and collaboration does not appear to "come naturally." None of us is programmed to use collaboration as our primary conflict resolution strategy. It's a strategy we learn to use throughout our lives.

Chart 12

Strategies and Outcomes of Conflict Styles

Strategy	Outcome
Avoid	You lose/they lose
Accommodate	You lose/they win or You win/they lose
Compete	You win/they lose or You lose/they win
Compromise	You lose/they lose
Collaborate	You win/they win

The trouble with the four inherent strategies is that they don't permanently resolve conflict. At best, they merely delay the conflict for another day. At worst, they create bitter animosity between people—even family members—that can last a lifetime. Chart 12 indicates the results of the various strategies.

A Process for Dealing with Conflict

Unless a conflict is resolved using a win-win strategy, the aftermath only sets up the conditions for the next conflict. A model based on the work of Alan C. Filley explains how this five-phase process works (see Figure 11).

Phase One: Antecedent Condition
A source of conflict exists. Common sources for problems within partnerships include:

- *Ambiguous jurisdiction:* When boundaries are unclear, each party may stray into an area the other feels is reserved for him or her, causing a territorial dispute.

- *Conflict of interest:* Sometimes one's interest is in direct conflict with the other's interest—for instance, both want the same piece of land.

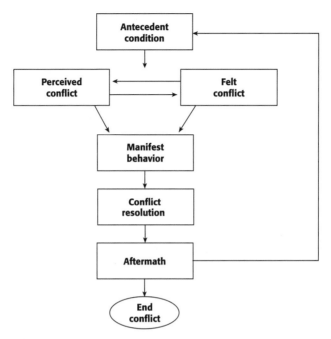

Figure 11   The Conflict Resolution Process

Adapted from Filley, 1975.

- *Communication barrier:* One is unable to communicate openly with the other. The source could be a language barrier (one speaks English, the other Spanish) or an organizational barrier (one is prevented from talking to the vice president of a company).

- *Dependence of one party:* One is dependent on the other to get his or her needs fulfilled. These needs can include information, resources, or support. Conflicts may increase if the other person withholds support or determines "what it is I need." The greater the dependence I have on you, for instance, the greater the potential for conflict.

- *Departmentalization within organization:* The greater the number of levels or departments in an organization, the greater the chance you'll be unable to resolve a conflict with the source. This is especially true if the problem exists at lower levels and people at the top make the decisions. When marketing makes decisions for production—for example, committing to a certain delivery date—

they may miscalculate the costs of inventory or labor, the availability of resources, and other essential factors.

- *Association of parties:* The people most distant from those who make decisions may understand the decision the least well. People outside "the loop" may fail to appreciate the issues involved in a particular conflict. They may discount the importance of a decision someone else sees as critical. A manager may not disagree with another manager about a decision, for example, but a line employee may.

- *Need for consensus:* Consensus requires all parties to agree on a resolution. When consensus is achieved, conflicts are resolved using a win-win strategy—thus preempting future conflicts.

- *Behavior regulations:* The greater the number of regulations on behavior, the greater the number of potential conflicts. Conflicts result when people make rules for others without consulting them.

- *Unresolved prior conflicts:* Unresolved conflicts will always resurface—even if the new conflict seems to involve a different issue.

Phase Two: Perceived/Felt Conflict

Once a conflict is in motion, people perceive something is wrong. Perception and feeling reinforce each other. Perception occurs in our minds and is a cognitive process. Maybe we think we notice a difference in someone's behavior toward us or in their tone of voice. Perhaps we perceive that a person is starting to avoid us because he or she doesn't return our telephone calls. This perception generates a feeling that alerts us we may be in a conflict situation.

The reverse can also happen. Sometimes we may *feel* that something is not quite right and then begin to think we notice changes in a person's behavior toward us. The gut (our feelings) reinforces what the mind (our perception) is telling us. Once we align our perception and our feelings, we achieve homeostasis—internal balance—and are *convinced* a conflict is occurring. And once we are convinced conflict exists (whether it does or not), we set in motion a complex set of dynamics. These dynamics manifest through verbal and nonverbal behavior that alerts the other to the conflict. Frequently the other party is already aware of it, having sensed a subtle change in behavior toward him or her. What we do then reinforces the other's perception of conflict or feeling of conflict.

I once witnessed a conflict between two employees, Carole and Tom, over how to design a workshop. Carol was the director of a communication company's organizational effectiveness group. Tom was a course designer. Carole and Tom had a difference of opinion on how to structure a workshop on internal partnerships. Although Carole eventually gave in to Tom's design, she confided to me she was uncomfortable with the way Tom had set up the breakout groups. She thought the two groups should meet separately, before the joint meeting, to discuss their needs privately. Tom wanted to bring the two groups together on the first day and mutually explore their needs. A day or two after Carole told me about the disagreement, Tom told me his perception. He thought Carole was avoiding him and failing to make eye contact with him when they talked.

Several days later, Tom told me he was getting a feeling that Carole was sabotaging the workshop. This feeling was reinforced, he said, when Carole mentioned she didn't care for the way he had designed the breakout groups. He said he had noticed Carole leaving a meeting with the organization's vice president (a meeting to which he hadn't been invited). He'd also heard a rumor that the workshops were to be canceled. When he confronted Carole about his perception, he felt there was a conflict between them. She immediately told Tom he wasn't listening to her comments on the workshop design. She said she felt ignored. Tom apologized and asked her if they could talk about the design and take another look at the breakout groups. After talking, they agreed to change the design of the workshop. Tom began to see the value of having each partner work independently of the other and then bringing their needs together. The workshop was a huge success, and Carole and Tom won a major award for their design. Ultimately they collaborated on the workshop design instead of fighting over it—and they both came out winners.

Phase Three: Manifest Behavior
After you've perceived and felt a conflict, it begins to influence your behavior toward others. Carole avoided Tom and wouldn't look him in the eye. Without consciously choosing a strategy to manage conflict, they probably would have reverted to their primary strategy for coping with conflict. People always revert to some form of fight or

flight response during the immediate aftermath of the conflict event. Unless we consciously opt for collaboration, we end up with temporary solutions that are not win-win.

Phase Four: Conflict Resolution

Once you've acknowledged a conflict, you need to decide how to resolve it. You can allow it to follow its natural course and use your innate strategy without thinking. Or you can choose to resolve the conflict through collaboration in order to achieve a better and more permanent resolution. Using a collaborative strategy means you invite the other along to resolve the conflict in a way that will create mutual satisfaction.

Phase Five: Aftermath

How you choose to resolve the conflict will determine the aftermath. If you've chosen any strategy other than collaboration, you have, in effect, set up the situation for the next conflict. And the "winner" of the original conflict is often the party that is blindsided later. Because they "won," they haven't a clue how the losers are feeling. Losers don't forget; they get even, and the cycle continues. But when conflict is resolved using a win-win strategy, there are no losers—and, consequently, the conflict is settled. A collaborative resolution precludes more conflict based on past grievances.

Conflict: The Dynamo for Synergy

In the example of Carole and Tom, the conflict created energy and they used that energy to create something better than they had at the start. They did so by creating a situation in which both of them won. Successful businesses know how to create win-win situations, too, whether they involve employees, departments, suppliers, or their customers. With the rapidly accelerating pace of change, companies that can transform conflicts into win-win situations will have an invaluable competitive edge. And organizations with a high PQ will have this skill.

CHAPTER TWELVE

Comfort with Interdependence

Learning the Virtues of Interdependence

Many companies throughout the world have established corporate cultures that are independent. In the past, independent organizations could succeed simply because the work done and the products produced did not require teamwork. In fact, organizational experts boldly reduced work to its simplest component in the never-ending quest for efficiency. As a result, organizations became more independent and more self-sufficient.

When Henry Ford developed his concept of mass production of automobiles, he built many related industries to provide the components for his cars. To manufacture the steel, he shipped taconite and iron ore to Michigan; to make the fabric for the upholstery, he built mills; to make the windows, he built glass plants. Each worker made or attached a part on the assembly line as the chassis flowed through the system. Today, however, robotic systems have replaced hundreds of thousands of these workers because they do the job better, faster, and more accurately, and they don't need health insurance.

Today in the United States, a company using its workforce as Ford did would find it tough to stay afloat. Such labor intensity would be too expensive. And besides, people are generally more educated today and want work that's more meaningful. What robots can't do is the creative, team-oriented work, which requires sophisticated communication and decision making. Managing creative teams is different from managing mechanical processes. Consequently, when the way the workforce is used begins to change, then management's thinking needs to change. In many organizations, however, workers are consistently asked to change and upgrade their skills—only to be directed by people using the same style of management that was in vogue fifty years ago.

THE TROUBLE WITH INDEPENDENCE

Management's job today is to build partnerships within organizations. In an information-based economy, no single group can be the sole purveyor of the "raw material" needed to manufacture the product.

Let me cite an example. I once worked with two partners who were in the mortgage banking business. In the mortgage business there are many players who each have a specialized role. There are closers who close a real estate transaction, lenders who loan the money, mortgage servicers who handle the loan, and mortgage custodians who manage the documents. This case involved mortgage servicers and mortgage custodians. The servicers handle customer calls, accept and apply payments, and pay escrowed taxes and insurance for the mortgagee. The custodians file and store the documents and then, when they're needed, ship them to appropriate locations—a cumbersome process considering the thousands of real estate transactions that occur every day.

The mortgage servicer company I worked with was frustrated with the custodian's tracking system. Frequently the servicer company would inquire where the documents were located and the custodian couldn't tell them. The firm of mortgage custodians felt they had a good process for identifying and retrieving documents and didn't want to hear complaints from the servicer. Nancy, the custodian CEO, told me, "Those mortgage servicers are never happy, no matter what we do!" In time, however, this servicer got a bad reputation among closers and lenders. It seemed that every time there was a closing and this particular company was involved, documents arrived late—causing late closings, scheduling nightmares, and angry buyers and sellers. Gradually closers and lenders started to avoid this servicer. When I discussed the issue with Bob, the servicer CEO, he said the custodian was trying to drive them out of business. I thought this a bit paranoid—

especially since Nancy, the custodian leader, had told me several times she had tried to improve the situation between the two groups. But, Nancy said, "mortgage servicers just aren't interested in partnering to fix the process."

At this point a vice president at the mortgage servicer urged me to work on improving their process. The first thing I did was bring the servicer and custodian together to talk about the tracking issue. After several meetings, we agreed to try working together to integrate their two processes. Using the Partnership Continuum model, we started off by defining the need. Once both parties agreed that the need was to get the correct document delivered to the correct location in time for the closing, we created a vision for the partnership. We then started on the initial activity: to document the two organizations' processes, set standards, and create a measurement system. After several months, the firm of mortgage servicers was able to improve its on-time delivery to closers by 200 percent. After one year, it had one of the best records in the business. Bob later confided that initially he hadn't believed we'd improve things. He'd felt that the custodians had spent too much money on their delivery system without consulting customers and that they would never change it. But partnering with the custodian and creating a sense of interdependence proved otherwise.

The independent system of doing business no longer works. Today the workplace rallying cry is teamwork. Organizations are becoming interdependent and relying on others to help them accomplish their goals. They're moving toward more openness and creating organizational cultures that support it. The Partnership Continuum model helps you assess where you are in this transition. As a partnership develops, it moves from being closed and solitary to being open and interdependent. By building relationships based on trust and by producing mutual benefits, the partnership can be long lasting.

INTERDEPENDENCE: WAVE OF THE FUTURE

Interdependence means two (or more) independent entities working together as partners without losing their separate identities. Interdependent partnerships succeed because each party needs assistance in achieving its goals and each contributes to satisfying the needs of the other partner. Approaching a partnership with the hope of simply buying a needed capability is not only shortsighted and naïve. It can have dire consequences.

I once worked with a telecommunications company whose mission included the goal "to maximize our stock portfolio." The leadership decided this meant they should partner with a financial institution in order to manage its portfolio more efficiently. What they needed was a partner to help them—an investment bank—but what they did was acquire a bank and attempt to run it themselves. The phone company tried to run the bank the same way it ran its phone operations—and the bank's operations suffered. The telecommunications leadership could not adjust to the fast pace with which decisions have to be made in financial institutions. Interest and currency markets can change almost hourly. The telecommunications firm, used to a slower pace due to regulatory bureaucracy, just couldn't make decisions fast enough. More important, its mission of maximizing its portfolio was distorted by the idea that it should manage this function itself.

After spending millions of dollars purchasing the bank and subsidizing its operations, the phone company sold it at a loss of many more millions of dollars. Because this was not a true partnership, it failed. Taking over is not partnering; it's a conquest. The structure of the partnership should preserve both partners' ability to contribute to the other. If your partner loses independence or can't maintain a separate identity, your partnership ceases to exist.

Northwest Airlines and KLM decided what they wanted from each other and used the term *alliance* to describe their relationship. They structured their partnership as interdependent—that is, maintaining two separate corporate identities but acting as a single company in the eyes of their customers. So they:

- Code-share, which allows them to book reservations on each other's flights using a single reservation system and flight numerics
- Share ticket check-in and baggage loading facilities
- Share catering services
- Share warehouse capabilities
- Purchase materials jointly, which reduces cost through volume
- Market jointly and cross-sell into each other's territory

This principle of maintaining interdependence is more difficult to envision when the companies working together are in different fields. When a partnership involves two different businesses, each partner's needs and capacities must be spelled out. McDonald's founder Ray Kroc was famous for partnering with the suppliers for his growing business. His business was selling fast food to millions of consumers, building restaurants, and investing in real estate. Even though he could have bought out the entire operations of many of his suppliers, he didn't. He wanted to maintain partnerships, believing that people who owned their own business were more productive. He went so far as to insist he pay a fair price to his suppliers rather than squeezing them for bare-bones concessions, which he could have done.

Kroc's dedication to maintaining interdependence was most evident in his decision not to sell vast exclusive territories for multiple franchises. Despite the attractiveness of huge up-front profits in selling off rights to big syndicates, he believed the owner-operator was the best operator. He knew "hands-on" owners would care about the business, not just about the numbers. His policy was to award only one restaurant at a time to an owner-operator. If that one was successful, the franchisee could apply for another. This is how Kroc's empire grew. Product, service, and operations were so good that McDonald's never worried about finding people who wanted their own cash machine.

McDonald's has continued to form alliances for marketing purposes—most notably with the Disney Corporation. For ten years these two giants have had a global alliance wherein McDonald's has promoted Disney movies. Not only did McDonald's promote four major film releases in 1998, but McDonald's is a sponsor of Dinoland at Disney's Animal Kingdom in Florida and is building Ronald's Fun House at Disney World. Disney employees even sell McDonald's french fries at Disney World. These two corporations have joint philanthropic ventures, too, including the American Teacher Awards and Young Inventors Awards, and have jointly donated millions of dollars toward the purchase of "Sue," a *Tyrannosaurus rex* skeleton, by Chicago's Field Museum. Clearly the two corporations share common goals—not only in cross-promotion but in catering to similar constituencies. It appears to be a good fit for both.

In the early 1990s, I was consulting with a large telecommunications company. I was part of a team that developed a partnership between management and the union to improve the quality of work processes. When I asked the management and union representatives to describe the company's culture, I heard: "It's like living in the old Soviet Union." The number of times I heard that analogy made an impact on me. Since I knew none of these people had lived in the Soviet Union, I asked them to elaborate. They gave me this list:

- Autocratic management style
- Dictatorial decision making
- No meaningful input from employees
- Closed access to information (secretive)
- Mistrust among employees
- Resistance to change
- Motivation based only on self-interest
- Favoritism

Now contrast this list with the one that Jack Stack, General Manager of Springfield Remanufacturing, gave me. Stack lists these positive components of interdependence:

- Embracing change
- Development of trust
- Meaningful contributions to decision making by employees
- Open management style
- Fewer employee problems
- Win-win conflict resolution

According to Stack, Springfield's success is based on attributes that are the exact opposite of those listed by the phone company employees. While the telecommunications company is still in business, it's a regulated monopoly. And, not surprisingly, it is clinging to its monopolistic practices by introducing lawsuits to prevent competition from entering its local service market. Clearly its management realizes the company could never compete in an open market, and so they're investing as much as they can into maintaining independent status quo.

No one at the telephone company intended to ignore the ideas of employees. But it's no mystery what the company really values: control. Adopt a past orientation, maintain the status quo, resist change—and you'll get a disgruntled workforce, poor productivity, and ultimate loss of control.

BREAKING THE OLD PARADIGM

Independent organizations that have not developed partnerships have systemic paradigms. If one part of the organization's culture—especially the leadership—is based on a paradigm of independence, then it's probable that other parts of the organization are driven by a similar dynamic. Organizational structures tend to replicate themselves. Like families that are influenced by the beliefs of the parents, organizations incorporate the values of their leaders. If the leadership is afraid to establish a partnership based on trust and mutual benefits, other parts of the organization will reflect that fear.

Leadership's values determine the organization's past or future orientation as well. Within that orientation lies a collection of attitudes and behaviors that reflect the company's culture. Owners and managers set the company's policies and establish independent or interdependent systems. If your company has a past orientation, it's hard to change direction. Even with an awareness of the problems, an intellectual understanding of the need for interdependence, a determination to undertake a fearless self-assessment, and a desire to change, most companies find changing a culture a slow and arduous process.

Assessing Management Style

The good news is that people can move from independence to interdependence. The first step is a realistic assessment of the management style practiced in the organization today (Survey 5). Do you frequently hear the phrase "I don't care what you think. I'm the boss—so just do it!" where you work? This type of statement, and the thinking and culture behind it, is death to a business and to the possibility of partnerships.

Interpreting the Results

Once you've completed Survey 5, tally up the totals in the yes and no columns. How many no's did you get? If you answered no to more than three questions, you may want to think about the independent paradigm of your organization. When leaders value interdependence, they create an environment that encourages involvement. From the boardroom to the shop floor, the more people are involved, the more interaction occurs. With that interaction comes a sense that "we are all in this together," and information starts to flow freely. The free

Survey 5. Independent or Interdependent?

Instructions

Review the eight statements listed below. Based on your position in the organization, answer yes or no to each statement. Sometimes the answer might be maybe. However, for the purpose of this exercise, think about what happens most of the time, especially during times when the organization is under stress. Then circle the most honest answer. This exercise provides helpful insight into the organization's comfort with interdependence when distributed to several layers of management and employees.

	Circle One	
1. I feel like a team member in my department.	Yes	No
2. Executives act on my input before decisions are made.	Yes	No
3. I work with my suppliers to resolve issues that affect both of us.	Yes	No
4. Important financial, strategic, and operational information is regularly provided to me.	Yes	No
5. Executives allow the workers closest to the job to make decisions affecting them.	Yes	No
6. My supervisor encourages me to work closely with other departments in this organization.	Yes	No
7. I am involved in my organization's strategic or functional planning.	Yes	No
8. When I have a cross-functional problem with other departments in our organization, they are willing to help resolve it.	Yes	No
Total Score:	_____	_____

exchange of information is fundamental to the success of organizations and a cornerstone to creativity. An organization that creates this kind of environment—one that build trust and eliminates fear—moves beyond competition into the zone of creativity and synergy.

Now that you've assessed where your organization stands in relation to independence and interdependence, here are some simple strategies to help you break out of the independent paradigm.

- Walk around the office and talk to employees.

- Hold a company retreat and ask for an honest assessment of the organization and its culture.

- Listen to the staff and act on their ideas.

- Go talk to your customers and ask them what they think of your organization.

- Establish open communication using a variety of avenues to solicit ideas and collect comments.

- Tell your employees what they have told you. Then they'll know you are listening.

FROM INDEPENDENCE TO INTERDEPENDENCE

An important skill in helping organizations move from independence to interdependence is the ability to achieve consensus. It's important because consensus drives collaboration between partners. The purpose of using a consensus style of decision making is to create win-win scenarios. Consensus decision making means that all parties feel confident about group decisions and are able to communicate, justify, and defend those decisions to their constituencies. People achieve a consensus decision through various means; no single way is gospel. When I work with a group, we discuss consensus. Then we build an agreement of what consensus decision making means for this group. This gives the group an opportunity to build a group norm and practice the concept we've just discussed. Some steps to use when implementing a consensus decision-making style include:

- List the mutual goals of the partnership (interest-based needs and wants).

- Identify issues that may prevent the partnership from achieving these goals.

- Establish boundaries for working toward the shared goals.

I've worked with many organizations to implement what I call interest-based problem solving. One such client was the Waldorf Corporation, headquartered in St. Paul, Minnesota. This company makes packaging for huge corporate clients from Land O'Lakes to Legos and from 3M to Hormel. They recycle paper products and work with governments around the globe in wastepaper recycling efforts. Dedicated to forging partnerships with clients the world over, management has also formed partnerships with four unions in an effort to foster win-win relationships. Their interest-based activities have focused on prioritizing and then finding ways to satisfy the interests of each side.

The interest-based approach was also used with the Dairyland Power Cooperative in Wisconsin in 1995 to negotiate agreements between unions and the company management. In this case the goal was to transform the mission statement originally approved by the labor/management committee in 1992 into a reality. Essentially both sides were bound by an agreement to use "interest-based bargaining/consensus" guidelines to resolve grievances, make decisions, and find the best solutions. This negotiating framework contains six important points.

First: Parties will achieve resolution through their joint efforts to discover the best solution. Communication skills are critical. We helped people become better listeners by focusing on a few steps:

- *Pay close attention to what others are saying.* Don't allow yourself to be distracted by outside influences. Look at your partners when they are talking. Be open to what they're saying and resist thinking of a retort while they're talking. After they've spoken, mentally count to ten while you consider how you want to respond. Then respond.

- *Ask clarifying questions.* Try not to compete with your partner. Rather, start by asking clarifying questions: "When you said let's meet for lunch, I thought you meant at twelve noon. Is that right?" By clarifying, you aren't forcing your partner to be defensive, but are simply requesting more information.

- *Paraphrase back to the speaker.* Using your own words, repeat what you thought you heard the speaker say. Then ask the speaker if he or she feels you understood the point.

- *State only your point of view.* Good ideas support themselves. People don't need to justify their opinions. Resist the temptation to criticize or comment on others' perspectives. Just allow them to state what they believe without offering anything more.

- *Don't discredit the views of others.* There's no need to discredit others' opinions. Their opinions are as important to them as yours are to you. By discrediting others, we only cause harm and resentment in the relationship. Reasonable people can disagree and still respect each other.

• *Limit discussion to the issue, not the person.* Keep the conversation focused on ideas. Don't succumb to attacking the speaker personally. The most effective way to resolve differences is to focus on facts, not on what we think the speaker intends.

Second: The solution must be acceptable to all the parties. When people with diverse points of view agree, the result is especially strong. By valuing differences, creative solutions arise. Different points of view and sources of information help the group expand, clarify, and define the issue in a way no one person can do. When we consider diverse opinions, we create synergy within the partnership.

Third: Any of the parties may block a potential decision. But the party blocking the decision must search for alternatives with the rest of the group. If an alternative solution is not forthcoming, the blocking party must reevaluate his or her position. Don't tolerate an irresponsible blocker. A person who blocks group consensus without offering a different perspective is acting in a passive/aggressive manner. The group needs to confront blockers and find out what they need to allow the group to move ahead. If they're unable to respond, it's best to table the issue for a period of time to allow them to come up with a different suggestion or rally behind the proposed resolution.

Fourth: Voting, horse trading, and compromise are not part of the process. As tempting as it may seem, do not vote, flip a coin, calculate an average, or use any other tension-reducing technique. Consensus decision making encourages divergent ideas to surface and allows conflicts to be resolved in an open manner. By using an averaging technique, we prevent the conflict from surfacing. This simply causes the conflict to resurface later—perhaps in a more destructive way.

The purpose of consensus is to find win-win outcomes. When we trade support or seek compromise, we're creating situations in which people may feel they've lost something. The idea is to find the best possible solution, not just to manufacture a conclusion. The sheer act of "sticking to it" creates a sense of trust between group members.

Fifth: Look for the best decision based on the available information. Once an issue has surfaced, gather as many facts about it as possible.

This allows the group to make a decision based on information rather than emotion. When information is lacking, the imagination takes over. So base your decisions on facts. Everyone should share information with the rest of the group. This is an effective method for building trust and ensuring that the consensus process generates the best decision possible.

Sixth: Both parties should focus on discovering the best decision within the context of the partnership while at the same time satisfying the interests of all major stakeholders. We identify areas where we agree and begin to build consensus from there. It's must easier to start from where we agree than from where we don't.

Once partners have worked through this process, they not only have achieved their desired outcome but have evolved toward a full partnership because they've become smarter partners. Although Dairyland obtained a negotiated contract that everyone praised as a breakthrough event, in fact everyone gained much more. The partnership not only created security for the union membership but provided new opportunities for expansion and growth for the cooperative.

People who believe they're being treated fairly are more productive. Those who believe their interests are being addressed feel valued and important. They feel part of a team, and they'll invest their time and energy in helping that team succeed. What accomplishes such enthusiasm is not a contract-signing ceremony but the process that produced the desired outcome. It is a powerful dynamic, one too often overlooked by businesses today. Once more, then, here are the ground rules for consensus:

- Create an environment that is open and trusting.
- Develop criteria for deciding when consensus has been achieved.
- Allow differences to surface.
- Respect each person's idea. You don't have to agree with it.
- Don't evaluate ideas until all suggestions are on the table.
- Evaluate ideas based on merit and information.
- Create win-win solutions.
- Discuss ideas until consensus has been achieved. Don't rush the discussion. Don't resort to voting or horse trading.

CHAPTER THIRTEEN

Ability to Trust

Creating Trust in Your Partnership

Of all the dynamics involved in partnering, I believe trust is the single most important. Trust is a result of what you and your partner do. It cannot exist without interaction. It isn't something you can bestow on another; it isn't a commodity that you can transfer. Trust is created when expectations are satisfied. It is destroyed when we experience disappointment. Either way, for more or less trust to exist, we have to view it as relational.

MAKING TRUST POSSIBLE

Three criteria make trust possible: telling the truth, taking the time to develop a relationship and explore each other's needs and expectations, and being personally accountable for doing what you promise.

Telling the Truth

Most of us in business don't intend to lie to our partners. But we sometimes avoid telling the whole story to be polite or perhaps to hide something unflattering to ourselves. Telling the truth means facing up to reality. Don't put a spin on matters of importance. Don't exaggerate what you're willing to do or contribute. The assessing stage of the Partnership Continuum cannot succeed without this kind of healthy self-view. You need to be strong enough to admit mistakes, acknowledge weaknesses, and ask for help. The more truth you both can share, the more trust you'll develop.

"Open book" management—an innovative style being used at many successful organizations—relies on the free flow of information up and down the corporate hierarchy to encourage creative solutions to problems and generate great new ideas for reducing costs and expanding the business. The idea that employees have an equity interest in the company means they have a right to know about every aspect of the business— from financial information to strategic marketing initiatives.

At Springfield Remanufacturing, one of the businesses currently using open book management, employees have an equity investment— and this style of operating is consistent with the owners' interests. If company owners share their profit motive with workers, then they'll profit, too. Jack Stack, the company founder, believes so strongly in partnering with all workers that he's instituted bonus plans, contests, and ongoing incentives for everyone's positive contributions to the company's bottom line. Sharing hitherto "company secrets" with all members of the company, as appropriate, is telling the truth. Stack's business is quickly dispelling the myth that employees cannot deal with the truth.

Taking the time

No matter how many times I say "relationship building takes time," I continue to encounter the client who wants to skip this step and "get on with the task." I have to reply: "This is the task."

The greater the trust level a partnership has created, the less need there is for maintenance. Relationships that are characterized by high intimacy but require little maintenance are usually long-term relationships. Some people I care about very much I hardly see, maybe once every four or five years. Yet when we are reunited, we carry on as if we've never been apart. It doesn't matter what we've done, where we've been, or what's happened in the intervening years. We immediately revert to our old trust level. Trust is the result of the time we spend building it; it can't be wished on a relationship.

Contrary to what may seem logical, conflict resolution builds trust. It is through working out our differences—by helping each other create win-win solutions—that we get to know each other's needs. We build goodwill by hanging in there and solving interpersonal and task-related problems. The success of the partnership is worth our efforts. Relationships that haven't experienced conflict haven't had the opportunity to grow stronger through the investigation of each other's needs and expectations. They haven't been given the chance to demonstrate mutual support and carry through the resolution of a problem—the building blocks of trust. These are human interactions that create mutual benefits and trusting relationships. They are not transactions to be bought and sold on a whim.

Being Accountable

The accountability factor in building trust relates to your own actions. You can't control what someone else does, but you *can* control what you do. If you're sensing uneasiness or an awkward feeling with a partner, ask yourself: "What can I do?" You can move along the Partnership Continuum by attending to your own accountability. The law of reciprocity—that is, others tend to give back what they have been given—works in building trusting relationships. One of my friends signs his e-mail with this slogan: "No act of kindness is ever wasted." In everything we do, intention is important—especially if that intention is "other-directed." Trust is an outcome of our inputs. Even the smallest gesture that is intended to be giving, respectful, supportive, encouraging, or sympathetic adds value to a relationship.

Building trust should be an intentional activity. And since the development of trust is such an essential aspect of successful partnerships, organizations should support its development. This takes planning. People intending to enter partnerships must engineer their performance so that they'll do what it takes to increase trust. When we care enough to plan, follow through, evaluate, and redirect our energies if necessary, we're using our partnering intelligence.

BUILDING TRUST

Suppose you want to develop a partnership with someone in whom you have little trust. You can make it work by understanding how to build trust and then taking the risks necessary to do so. Trust is the key to your ability to move into the creative zone of true synergy. In the creative zone, people and organizations achieve their highest potential. The best partnerships move toward this outcome.

It takes a two-pronged approach to discuss trust with your partner. First, you need to understand your own ability to trust. Since humans run the whole range from full trust to no trust, it's best to have a realistic assessment of your own beliefs about trust. Second, after assessing your trust level, you can turn to the trust level between partners. Understanding your partner's ability to trust and assessing his or her current level of trust is an important benchmark in the stages of relationship development. If you can honestly say that you trust each other, then you only need to build on that trust. But if you are partnering with someone you do not trust, acknowledging that fact openly is a big step toward establishing future trust. Let's start with assessing ourselves first. Take a few moments to answer the Personal Trust Questionnaire (Survey 6).

FIVE KEY INGREDIENTS FOR TRUST

Think about building trust as a process—like baking a cake. The better the ingredients you put into the recipe (inputs), the better the cake (output). So too, with trust. Below are five key ingredients (inputs) that will help you create trust (output) in your partnerships.

Be Open, Honest, Direct

Examine your own level of trust—both in general and specifically toward your partner. Are you a trusting person? If not, can you say that to your partner openly and objectively? Tell him or her the impact his or her actions had on you. Be open, honest, and direct. The more straightforward you are, the more therapeutic it will be for both you and your partner. Though this may be an uncomfortable exercise, it will help take your partnership to a higher trust level.

Focus on Your Behavior

Remember the old saying: "Walk the talk." This means that most people are watching our actions much more closely than our words. What do you want to project in your actions? You can engender a trustful response if you follow through on your promises. You can gain your

Survey 6
Personal Trust Questionnaire

Instructions

Circle your personal rating for each question and add up the total

Personal Trust Questionnaire	Strongly Disagree ➤ Strongly Agree
	Circle One
1. General trust: In general, I am a trusting person.	1 2 3 4 5
2. Self-confidence: I trust myself to get the job done if that's what I've promised to do.	1 2 3 4 5
3. Trusting another: Specifically, with _____ I feel my trust level right now is very strong.	1 2 3 4 5
4. Situational point of view: I am less concerned about my past dealings with _____ than about what we will do from now on.	1 2 3 4 5 1 2 3 4 5
5. Willingness to confront my partner: I feel confident demanding accountability from my partner.	1 2 3 4 5

Scoring

Understanding ourselves enhances our insights into our relationships. If you scored less than 15 points on Survey 6, think about it and talk about it. If your lack of trust involves what your partner did, discuss your concerns with your partner. Concerning your rating on question 3, be specific: Exactly how does your partner's behavior make you feel? Stick to behavior itself rather than what you think motivated it. Above all, avoid making assumptions about honesty, integrity, or ethical judgment.

Statement	Points
1	
2	
3	
4	
5	
Total Score	

partner's respect if you are respectful in what you say and do. If you're issuing a written statement regarding the partnership, for instance, be sure to show it to your partner in advance. Ask your partner to help you write it. Before you speak, ask yourself whether your words will build trust in the partnership or destroy it. You will know the answer.

Focus on Your Feelings

When communicating in the partnership, you need to be aware of what is going on inside you. Are your suspicious feelings the result of what is happening now? Or is outdated information triggering your uneasiness? Is it what the other person is saying or doing that bothers you? Or are you basing your judgments on a negative experience in your past?

Talk It Out with Others

If a topic is emotional for you, talk it out. By talking with others you can learn about other perspectives that may be more objective than yours. Perhaps a new perspective can help you resolve the issue. Try to find someone who will listen to you without judging and help you focus on the real issue rather than the emotion. Once the issue is identified, try using a problem-solving approach directly with the other person. This task has the best chance of resolving most issues and creating win-win scenarios.

Just a caution: beware of "triangulating"—that is, using someone else to mediate for you. This leads to miscommunication and merely complicates issues. Never choose an indirect way of confronting. Approach the person yourself. By the time the partnership has broken down to the point of seeking third-party mediation, the level of trust has dissolved significantly. Mediators are useful when the relationship has to stay together—for instance, the relationship between a union and a company. In partnerships, however, the use of a third-party mediator is the equivalent of divorce court. Asking a friend to help you reach a decision is very different from involving a third party in the partnership. It never hurts to bounce ideas off someone else to check for validity. But don't ask that person to speak for you. And refrain from criticizing your partner. It can only undermine the partnership.

Stop the Action

If you're feeling uncomfortable during a meeting, stop the task and tell your partner how you're feeling. You can address what's bothering you, and then you can focus on the task once more. Feeling uncomfortable with how the partnership is proceeding is probably a relationship issue. Discomfort and weak communication skills go hand in hand. Work on better communication and the whole partnership will improve.

THINKING ABOUT TRUST

Past and future orientation are environments that foster or destroy trust. (See Chart 13.) When a person or organization has a past orientation, their outlook will destroy trust.

Once you've completed your personal assessment of trust using the Personal Trust Questionnaire (Survey 6), you may want to ask yourself some questions:

- What am I currently doing to build or destroy trust in the partnership?
- What did my partner do today to build or destroy trust between us?
- Did I have to hide something from my partner today?
- How did I communicate trust to my partner?
- What can I do to increase the level of trust in our partnership?
- What can my partner do?

Assessing Trust Within the Partnership

Now that you've answered these questions, it's time to think about trust within the partnership itself. One method of continuing to focus on the trust issues is to talk about them. This is the purpose behind the Partners' Trust Questionnaire (Survey 7). You and your partner should fill out this questionnaire separately and then discuss your responses.

Chart 13

Impact of Orientation on Trust

Past Orientation (−)	Future Orientation (+)
Reliance on past history for decision making removes the possibility for change and destroys trust.	Reliance on mutual vision and strategic planning for decision making increases trust by allowing partners to jointly create the vision and strategy, set goals and objectives, and measure their progress.
Independent behavior destroys trust because spontaneous actions occur without communication and feedback between partners, thereby increasing suspicion.	Interdependent behavior increases trust by creating mutual needs. When people are working together to satisfy their mutual needs, trust is generated.
Maintaining the status quo reduces trust. When partnerships are created, change is a natural result; when others cannot accommodate that change, trust is destroyed.	Seeking creativity and mutual benefits by embracing change creates trust. When people benefit by the outcome, trust is enhanced. When people have the opportunity to participate in the change process, trust increases.
Win-lose conflict resolution and problem solving destroys trust. Partners on the losing end will feel their concerns are not valued in the partnership.	Win-win conflict resolution and problem solving instills trust. Partners see their concerns being acted on in a positive manner.
High need for control destroys trust. When people insist on controlling a situation, they do not seek input from others. Partners who are out of the information loop have low trust due to the lack of information.	Low need for control builds trust. With a low need to control, partners ask freely for input. When people are solicited for their ideas and see them put into practice, their trust increases.
Closed systems destroy trust. When people feel others are hiding the truth, the result is mistrust.	Open systems create trust by allowing free access to information. With the necessary data, people can make their own decisions.

Survey 7
Partners' Trust Questionnaire

Instructions

This questionnaire reveals the overall perception of trust by members of the partnership. Circle your response to each statement.

Partners' Trust Questionnaire	Never	Sometimes	Often	Frequently	Always
			Circle One		
1. I feel a high level of trust in this partnership.	1	2	3	4	5
2 There is a high level of trust between the members of this partnership.	1	2	3	4	5
3. I believe the partnership helps me meet my needs.	1	2	3	4	5
4. I believe I help my partners meet their needs.	1	2	3	4	5
5. It's easy for me to express my needs to the partners.					

Scoring

After you and your partner have completed the questionnaire, review and discuss your results. Be as open, honest, and direct as you can. The more straightforward you are, the more trust you will build in your partnership.

You may want to focus on any statement on which you scored 3 or less.

Statement	Points
1	
2	
3	
4	
5	
Total Score	

Interpreting the Results

Once you've completed the Partners' Trust Questionnaire (Survey 7), you may want to discuss some questions as a way to debrief the activity.

- What surprised you about the responses?
- What did you like about the responses?
- What did you dislike?
- What do you think is the single biggest contributor to trust between partners?
- What do you think is the single biggest destroyer of trust?
- What have you done recently to build trust in your partnership?
- What have you done recently to destroy trust?
- If you had one single trust issue to work on, what would it be?
- Do you want to create an action plan to improve this situation?

Whenever you move from "I" to "we" in a partnership, trust issues emerge. Unless partners can reach a consensus, they'll find that power plays, egos, conflicting agendas, and other disruptive dynamics can take over even well-intentioned partnerships and spin them into chaos and dysfunction. Trust is absolutely essential for working through these complex human dynamics.

CHAPTER FOURTEEN

Self-Disclosure and Feedback

The Importance of Two-Way Communication

Robert is a district manager of a nationwide auto parts distributor. He was lamenting to me one day about how he was the last to hear about problems in the stores. "I know the store managers are trying to protect me from the day-to-day problems," he said, "but if I don't know what the issues are, how can I resolve them?" Ironically, just the day before, I had seen Robert explode at Allen, the manager of a suburban store, who had failed to set up a promotion display. It was two days before the sales campaign was to be released in the media. Allen tried to explain that the material had not yet arrived. This, he said, was an ongoing problem with market communications. But Robert didn't want to hear excuses. He upbraided the manager for not taking the initiative to find out where the material was. When Allen tried to comment, Robert just walked away. In fact, the manager had checked on the material earlier that morning and had been assured it would be delivered that afternoon in plenty of time.

That evening at dinner, I asked Robert about the episode with the store manager. "Robert, you complain that the store managers keep you in the dark, and yet I learned a very important piece of information today about your business. It sounds to me as if the market communications department has trouble getting promotion materials to your stores on time."

Robert thought about this for a minute and said: "If our store managers were more on the ball and checked on these things earlier, we wouldn't have this problem. I know Allen. He always waits till the last minute for everything."

"Wait a minute," I said. "Let me make sure I understand the issue here. You tell me that your employees keep you in the dark. Then we go and meet with a store manager who tells you about a problem he is experiencing and you get mad and blame *him* for the problem. Do you think there might be a connection here between employees not telling you something and how you reacted to that manager?"

"I don't think so," Robert stated tentatively.

"I see a big connection," I said. " When you ask for feedback and then jump on the person who provides it, you're creating a culture in which people don't want to tell you anything. They feel you'll just blame them. And so they keep the problems to themselves and try to fix them as best they can. And because these events happen in isolation from each other—the Northtown store doesn't know that Southdale is having the same problem—you can't attack the root cause and create a synergistic partnership with your store managers. Robert, you're going to have to create the kind of open communication and feedback that will help you gain the trust of your employees. And with that trust, you can develop partnerships with the store managers to run the business the way you've envisioned. But you have to let the managers disclose what the problems are in a safe and open environment. Otherwise, you'll just create an environment of fear."

Robert and I then explored other ways he could have handled that situation. Finally, Robert said, "I guess I've never thought about how I react before. I have a lot to learn about creating partnerships, haven't I?"

EXPRESSING YOUR NEEDS

An important element of partnering intelligence is the ability to express one's needs. In this section I present two tools that can help you increase your skill in this area: the JoHari Window and the Self-Disclosure Assessment. Both tools are easy to use and will give you insight into your ability to self-disclose.

Let us begin with the JoHari Window (Figure 12). This model demonstrates the limits of our self-understanding. The developers of

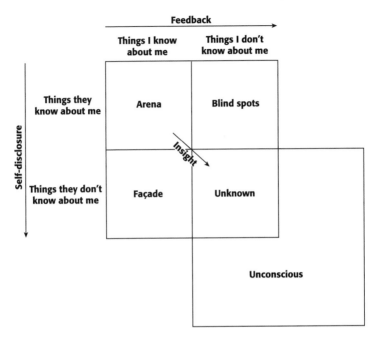

Figure 12   JoHari Window

this concept, Joseph Luft and Harry Ingham, each contributed part of his first name to the model—thus the name JoHari. Understanding how others see you and listening to what they have to say about you can confirm—or change—how you view yourself.

We all have *arenas*—open areas where we already share and learn from each other. You may know a lot about your partner because you work in the same office or live in the same house. The more you share, the closer you become. The most productive relationships occur when the arena is large and there's a balance between receiving feedback and self-disclosing. The arena should be large because it encompasses a large amount of information that is common to both of you. This will increase your opportunity to create synergy.

All of us also have *blind spots*—weaknesses that we can't see but others can. For instance, you might not realize that a phrase you use in an interview has a negative connotation for some people. If you're made aware of it, though, you will gladly stop using it. If your partner gives you that information to benefit the relationship, the trust level between you will be enhanced.

Exercise 13. Self-Disclosure Checklist		
Question	**Yes**	**No**
1. Is it difficult for you to talk to other people?		
2. Do you find it hard to express controversial ideas to those who may disagree with you?		
3. In a conversation, do others talk more than you?		
4. Do you refrain from talking about your personal life in business settings?		
5. Do you deliberately hide your weaknesses from others?		
6. Are you uncomfortable admitting mistakes to others?		
7. When you are with others, do you stick to business?		
8. Do you easily share your feelings with others?		

We also have a *façade*—a secret side that only we know about but that we could reveal to others to help them understand us. Disclosing information in an interview about your past experience in forming partnerships might help a firm decide you are right for them. They'd know that you have a track record and that your proposal works.

The fourth quadrant of the window is called the *unknown*—an area neither you nor your partner can know except by sharing information. The more you share, the smaller this area becomes. We also have our *unconscious*—an area not known to ourselves or to others.

As the façade and blind spots grow smaller through self-disclosure and providing feedback, the arena expands. With mutual disclosure, the unknown area shrinks as well. The goal of positive communication is to expand the arena by learning more about yourself from others' perspectives and sharing more information that may be unknown to others. In this way, more information is passed back and forth between you—creating new opportunities for synergy and creativity.

The second tool is the Self-Disclosure Checklist (Exercise 13). We typically don't give much thought to how well we self-disclose information to others. Exercise 13, the Self-Disclosure Checklist, provides you with an opportunity to reflect on how well you do this vital activity.

Choose a focus—work or home. Reflect on the question and answer it yes or no. If you think the anser is "sometimes" or "maybe," search deeper. How do you feel most of the time? The more honestly you can answer these questions, the more insights you will have into your ability to self-disclose information about yourself.

If you answered yes to three or more of the questions in Exercise 13, you may want to think about how freely you disclose information about yourself. While it isn't appropriate to share *everything* about your life, self-disclosure is essential in a partnership. The greater the self-disclosure, the more information flows and the more trust is established. It's better to provide too much information about yourself than not enough.

GIVING AND RECEIVING FEEDBACK

A client of mine, John, owns a medical supply company that specializes in selling different types of X-ray film in a highly competitive market. John continually gave his sales managers the message that every employee had to give 120 percent on the job. Numerous times he announced, too, that he expected at least a fifty-hour work week from each of his sales managers. That was what he did himself as a sales manager, and he expected no less from them. One afternoon Rick, a sales manager, came up to me and said he had had enough of John constantly telling him he wasn't working hard enough. In fact, Rick stated, "I lead the group in sales." Rick was a young man in his thirties, had two young children, and wanted to spend more time at home with his family. Not only were the long hours difficult for his wife, but he didn't have time to spend with the children. Even though he liked the work and loved the salary, he was thinking about quitting his job. "John's family is grown and he's divorced his wife," Rick said. "No wonder he's constantly riding our backs to do more and more. He has nothing else to live for! He needs to get a life!"

It was true. John's personal life was a mess. I had known John for twenty years and had seen him go through a bout with alcohol, leave his family several times, divorce his wife, and alienate himself from his children.

"Rick," I said, "have you confronted John with these complaints?"

"No, I haven't," he replied. "I'm petrified about how he would take it."

"Well, letting John know how you're feeling is pretty important," I noted. "He needs you. You like the work. It seems to me that you've got a situation in which both can win. Would you consider approaching him about forming a partnership and then discussing what both your needs are in this relationship? John wants to be sure that sales stay high. You want to spend time with your family. Aren't both things possible?"

"Well, I think so," he replied.

Later that week, Rick set up an appointment with John and asked me to join in.

Rick started off by saying he was very unhappy with the situation at work and was thinking about leaving. Although his sales were the highest in the district, he was working long hours and missing precious time with his family. His children, he said, were growing up in a fatherless household. Rick did an excellent job of disclosing his situation and feelings to John. Then he gave John some feedback: "John, you're constantly riding us to put in more hours. You're extremely demanding, and that makes me nervous. Sometimes I'm even afraid of you. I'm really having a problem with this coming from you on a weekly basis. I feel that you're unhappy in your personal life. You have divorced your wife, and your children don't want to see you. I don't want this to happen to me. Did you ever consider that what you are asking me to do is exactly what put you in the situation you're in today?" Rick said this in a calm, matter-of-fact manner. John turned red. He just sat there and stared out the window. I thought he was going to either explode or cry.

"I didn't know you felt this way," John finally mumbled. "I had no idea I was coming across as so demanding. It's just that I work hard and some of the managers don't seem to be pulling their weight. We've got to continue to grow our sales or we won't be getting the bonuses we've come to expect. I just never thought about how it might hit you on a personal basis. I've always tried to keep my personal life out of my business."

"John, I am a whole person. I cannot keep my personal life out of my business life. What you are asking me to do has an impact on my family and on me personally. I want to continue to work for you, but I can't do it the way things stand. I propose that you and I form a partnership. I think we should talk about what each of us needs from our partnership in order to be successful." The discussion soon turned to what these two business associates needed from each other to be successful.

About six months later, I ran into Rick at a meeting and asked him how things were going. He said he had formed a partnership with John and a little later was named a vice president of the sales department. John himself later told me that the meeting had been a turning point in his life. No one had ever confronted him about his demanding behavior before, and he had spent many hours reflecting on his life. After Rick took over the sales department, he asked me to help him establish internal partnerships with each of his sales associates. Over the next four years, their sales increased about 300 percent.

In Rick and John's case, John had been giving his sales managers the message that they weren't working hard enough. (This was John's perception of the situation.) This message reflected John's value of hard work and dedication to the job (providing insight into John's work ethic). Rick recognized that John's value of long hours was on a collision course with his own value of spending time with his family. Thus John's message provided Rick with two important pieces of information about John: his perception of what was happening and insight into his values.

Sometimes I ask myself certain questions when I'm in the process of providing feedback to another. You may want to think about the following questions the next time you're in a position to give someone feedback:

- Describe the behavior you want to comment on. What did the person do or say?
- How did his or her behavior affect you?
- How did you feel about what he or she did or said?
- How do you want to express the feedback to the other person?

Answer the questions in Exercise 14 to help you assess your ability to give and recieve feedback.

Giving Feedback

The ability to provide feedback within the context of partnership is an important aspect of your partnering intelligence. If you can't provide feedback, resentment begins to fester. As in conflict, a partner's

Exercise 14. Feedback Checklist		
Question	**Yes**	**No**
1. Are you comfortable providing feedback to others?		
2. Are you comfortable accepting feedback?		
3. When you give feedback, do you offer an example of the behavior?		
4. Do you ask people how they feel about what you just said?		
5. Do you provide feedback even if it might create conflict?		
6. When others hurt your feelings, do you tell them?		
7. Do you react calmly and nondefensively when someone gives you feedback?		
8. Do you help others understand you by saying what you think and how you feel?		
9. Do you let others finish before answering?		
10. When a person provides you with feedback, do you try to justify your behavior?		

resentment develops into passive-aggressive behavior that quickly turns destructive.

The best model I've seen for giving feedback has five basic steps:

1. You note a person's behavior.

2. The behavior creates an impression on you—maybe good, maybe bad, but powerful enough for you to take notice.

3. Time passes. You evaluate what you want to do about the impact of the behavior. If it's urgent, you may react immediately: "That was a great comment you made." Or "Please stop interrupting me." Depending on the situation, you may want to give the feedback in a private setting. In general, though, I recommend giving it as soon as possible after the behavior.

4. Present the feedback. Describe the behavior and tell the person the impact it had.

5. Decide what to do with the person's reaction. Remember: The feedback is yours. It's *your* impression that you're giving the

receiver. All you can do is provide people with feedback. It's up to them to decide what they want to do with the information.

There are two different methods for transmitting feedback: nonverbal and verbal. Nonverbal communication delivers about 80 percent of your message. Nonverbal cues—facial expression, body language, tone of voice, gestures, and so on—carry more weight, in fact, than your words. Most of us trust the nonverbal. We tend to believe what we see, not what we hear. When we decipher nonverbal communication, we tend to focus on three elements: the body, the voice, and our relationship with the speaker.

The way you use your body sends a message to the listener. What kind of message would you be sending if you told someone you care about him or her—but with a smirk on your face? If you were talking to someone and jabbed a finger into his or her shoulder, how would he or she receive your message? Eye contact delivers another powerful nonverbal message. In western society, if we don't look someone in the eye while talking to him or her, we may be transmitting a message of dishonesty or shame.

Your voice and tone transmit nonverbal messages, too. When someone is screaming at you, what are you thinking? Anger or urgency? It could mean either. When someone whispers, what does that mean? If you're listening to someone who is constantly saying "Ah," "Um," or "Uh," what do you think?

Yet another nonverbal message is conveyed by the way you position yourself physically in relation to the person. If you're standing over a seated person, how do you think the person feels? If you are a male seated at the head of the table, what kind of message do you think you are sending to the others at the table?

The second kind of feedback, verbal feedback, is what we actually say, either in person or in writing. How we provide verbal feedback may interfere with the message we want to deliver. Here are some tips to help you provide clear, concise, and effective feedback.

- Examine the reason why you are providing the feedback. Be sure that your intention is to help the other person, not to hurt him or her or to get even.

- Think about whether the person is ready to hear the feedback. If he or she is emotional or upset, will he or she really hear what you're saying?

- Offer the feedback as soon as you see behavior that troubles you. Immediate feedback is the most effective.

- Describe the behavior rather than evaluate it. For example: "Debbie, I just saw you roll your eyes when I told you I have a meeting. Don't you believe me?" is more effective than "You don't believe me, do you?"

- Be specific. Avoid the words *always* and *never.* People are complex beings and rarely engage in perfectly consistent behavior.

- Ask for permission to give feedback. Information is received more effectively when it's requested rather than imposed.

- Offer the feedback as a suggestion rather than an imperative.

- Be open to receiving feedback yourself. How did you contribute to the situation? What did the feedback say about your own behavior?

- Present one piece of feedback at a time. Too much information can overload people and cause them to reject all of it.

- Observe how the feedback is being received. Does the person accept it as genuine? Or is it something he or she doesn't believe?

- Don't offer feedback on behavior that people cannot change. If a person stutters, for example, you needn't offer feedback on it.

When giving feedback to someone, use specific examples that just now occurred. This way, the person will remember the incident and be able to relate to it. Try to provide the feedback using "I" statements. For example, "Neal, you just interrupted me while I was speaking; I get the feeling you're not listening to me."

Receiving Feedback

There is a skill in receiving feedback. Try to view it as a gift—a present someone is giving you. How you receive the feedback will determine the environment you set up for future feedback. Try to receive it with an open mind. Remember that you have a blind spot, too. That blind spot can be made smaller when feedback is accepted, validated, and appropriately acted upon. When you receive feedback, just listen to what the other person has to say. Then thank him or her for the feedback. He or she has just given you information. You don't need to act on it right away. Think about it. Ask yourself: Does this feedback fit me or not?

Exercise 15. Feedback Observation Checklist			
Was the Feedback . . .	**Yes**	**No**	**Comments**
1. Given with care?			
2. Focused on specific behavior?			
3. Given immediately?			
4. Delivered in an objective and nonjudgmental manner?			
5. Given directly to the person meant to receive it?			
6. Phrased with "I" statements?			
7. Excessive?			

Not all feedback is valid. Remember that feedback also reflects on the person providing it. He or she could be angry with you or the situation and be misdirecting his or her anger toward you in the form of feedback. Or he or she could have misinterpreted what occurred and why. Feedback given to you is in your control. You can decide whether or not you want to act on it.

Giving helpful feedback is a skill that requires practice. Rarely do we give feedback perfectly the first time. The Feedback Observation Checklist (Exercise 15) helps partners observe how well feedback is given. Pass the checklist out at the start of a partner meeting. Ask people to observe when feedback is given and determine whether the person providing the feedback was using the techniques listed. At the end of each meeting, conduct a team process check and review the Feedback Observation Checklist. This helps people open their arena by providing them with feedback on how they give feedback.

Your ability to self-disclose and to give and receive feedback is an important attribute in creating partnership. The more you can master this ability, the more you will increase your partnering intelligence.

CHAPTER FIFTEEN

Coming Full Circle

Hallmarks of a Successful Partnership

A partnership isn't valuable merely because it has the potential to be valuable. We err if we assume potential is destiny. In fact, most of a partnership's success depends upon human factors. The value of a partnership is the product of our combined potential vision, made real by our mutual inputs and nurtured through the human relationship. It's a process of giving, investing, contributing, and combining what we have to create synergistic results.

SIX HALLMARKS OF SUCCESS

The commitment we make to a full partnership is the commitment to continue to respect each other and honor the partnership as a special relationship. The evolving partnership has a life of its own and requires all of the same life-sustaining efforts and energies as any other enterprise. The special power of the partnership derives from the fact that it is created on purpose, it is sustained by conscious diligence, and it flourishes as a result of renewed commitment by the partners. The following six tenets are the key components that make a partnership work.

1. Active support of leaders

2. Appropriate team membership with equal participation

3. Common objectives

4. Clear boundaries and scope

5. Consensus and openness

6. Trust and mutual benefits

Active Support of Leaders

In organizational partnerships, the partners who initiated the alliance should be responsible to all the stakeholders who must make it work. The leaders who put together a merger of two companies, for instance, should keep selling the benefits of the partnership to their companies. They can do this by cheerleading, by providing financial resources for the transitions required, and by ensuring communication to the rest of the stakeholders. Most of all, leaders can send a supportive message by continuing their personal participation in efforts to ensure the success of the merger. Their participation must be visible so that everyone in the partnership understands that the leaders support the changes they are asking others to make.

I once consulted with an organization in which the top executives only paid lip service to the partnership. Although they spent no energy on developing it, they did stage a public relations campaign and receive recognition for being innovative. What they didn't do was show support for and participate in the changes they had instituted. Consequently, the partnership dissolved. Leadership's enthusiasm must be authentic; otherwise, people will feel exploited and withdraw their support.

Appropriate Team Membership with Equal Participation

When partnerships first develop, partners should share power. If one partner dominates the process, the dynamics of the alliance may become unbalanced. And stakeholders should participate all the way through the process. Stakeholders include everyone who will be affected by the partnership: production staff, clerical workers, salespeople, accountants, and others. If the organization is unionized, a representative from the union organization must be included.

Moreover, the partnership must be voluntary. If a critical person or group chooses not to participate, it should not prevent the partnership from forming. It simply means that some elements have not moved along the Partnership Continuum at the same rate as others. Remember the episode regarding the U.S. Postal Service? One of the largest unions refused to partner with management in order to improve the workplace environment. But that didn't stop managers from creating a partnership with others who shared a mutual interest. Like the Postal Service, you may want to keep the door open to potential partners who declined the initial offer. They may still have valuable insight and contribute to the overall success of the partnership.

The ability to participate equally often depends on being included in the loop. Equal access to information is necessary to ensure a level playing field between partners. If certain members of the partnership have exclusive access to information, it's incumbent on them to share it. They should make a point of including the other partners by forwarding copies, making memos, or instituting regular reporting regimens. Sharing information starts the process of building trust. If one partner hoards information, what message does this send to the other partners? Hoarding information sends a message of control, manipulation, and secrecy. It erodes confidence and destroys trust in the partnership. Another reason for sharing as much information as possible is that the "owner" of the data may get a new understanding of the information by having others look at it. If partners truly share mutual interests, what reason could there be to withhold relevant information from a partner?

Common Objectives

A partnership needs to identify the objectives of the relationship. For example, I worked in a manufacturing setting establishing a partnership between a company and its union. Their common objective was to grow the business. But growth required retooling the production line and increasing automation. While the company and union had a single common objective, each also had its own separate objectives. The company wanted to improve the production rate by 25 percent while reducing work defects by 10 percent. The union did not want the company to lay off employees in the process.

This group spent a lot of time and effort documenting their objectives and involving all the partners. Because of the documentation, all stakeholders understood the outcomes expected in the partnership. They could all see what was in it for them and the other parties if the alliance achieved its goals. Before I bring parties together and develop a mutual vision of the partnership, I have each group meet separately. In these separate meetings, they create their own vision of what they want from the partnership. Then I bring the parties together to share their individual visions. Inevitably the group begins to identify areas they have in common. That is the start of the mutual vision and the first step for creating common objectives.

Clear Boundaries and Scope

The partners need to define boundaries. Boundaries generally fall into the two dimensions of space and time. Space refers to what we agree to work on together. We may choose to work on one process improvement project, for example, and limit the partnership to that activity for now. Space may be limited to a function—for example, we may agree to work together in the manufacturing or marketing segment of the organization.

The other dimension is time. A time limit should be defined for the partnership—say one year or for the life of a contractual agreement. A formal agreement can be renegotiated when the time limit expires. This helps partners be more realistic about what they can commit to providing. The longer the time limit, the greater the risk that the partnership will not accomplish its objectives as planned. Being accountable now and planning what to do in the immediate future are more valuable to the partnership than making commitments based on fanciful predictions.

A group will take as long as a group has. Time is one of the most valuable commodities in organizational life, and scheduling timelines demonstrates respect for people's time. If there is no urgency, the partnership may run out of steam before it ever gets going. Setting timelines, milestones, or benchmarks keeps both the task issues and the relationship issues on track.

The first steps along the Partnership Continuum engage parties in a single activity to determine together the scope of their partnership. They need to decide what they expect from the partnership. How often will they need to work together? Will this be an ongoing relationship or will it be limited to just this project? If they work together in one area of their mutual interest, can they work together in other areas? Limiting the scope of a partnership may be much easier for strangers to accomplish than for familiar entities.

In a labor-management situation, for instance, a company may want to partner with its union to improve quality, productivity, or processes—yet it wants to be adversarial when it comes to negotiating benefits and wages. These two contrary positions may be difficult to understand. A true partnership needs to focus on mutual interests, but it doesn't have to encompass all the interests of both parties. Even in a labor-management dispute over compensation, the two sides can succeed in forging a partnership based on common objectives to resolve their dilemma.

After the partners have determined the scope of the partnership, they must communicate quickly and often to make sure both sides understand the limits of the partnership. My friend Larry works for an airline that recently offered its employees stock in the airline in exchange for pay cuts. The company broadcast its offer through the media—emphasizing the opportunity for employees to own the airline, just as management does with its stock ownership program. But Larry discovered he did not have the same benefits and privileges the managers had; while managers fly for free, the union employees pay a nominal fee for their passes. Larry resents the fact that while he takes stock instead of dollars, just like management, he doesn't enjoy the same treatment. The managers' free seats undermine the credibility of the public relations campaign aimed at building employee morale.

Had the airline been more precise with its employees and stated that it regarded the stock option as a different form of paycheck, perhaps my friend wouldn't feel so resentful. The airline overstated the scope of the partnership and inflated employees' expectations. A similar proposal may backfire in the future. The next time the labor contract is up for negotiation, employees may hold out for the money.

Consensus and Openness

A partnership based on trust and mutual benefit must have open communication between partners. Openness allows people to say what is in their hearts. This type of communication, while difficult for some, must be incorporated at every stage—especially at the storming stage.

Progress comes from working through conflicts. And in order to resolve conflicts, people need to work collaboratively.

The purpose of using a consensus style of decision making is to create win-win scenarios. By using some basic guidelines for consensus decision making, people embrace the technique because it ultimately enlists the enthusiasm of the whole team.

Trust and Mutual Benefits

The subtitle of Harvey Mackay's second book (1997) offers this advice: Do what you love, love what you do, and deliver more than you promise. There's no better way to develop a trusting partnership than to do more than the minimum your partner expects. Trust isn't automatic; it has to be earned. Trust levels are relative and can increase or decrease depending on what the partners do or don't do to build trust. If doing what you promise to do builds trust over time, exceeding your promises multiplies the impact of your actions.

We should try to exceed—rather than merely meet—the requirements of our promises. "Exceeding expectations" sounds like you expend full effort and enthusiastically complete the task, whereas "meeting requirements" sounds like you grudgingly perform the minimum. A law of physics states that for every action there is an equal and opposite reaction. Exceeding performance expectations triggers a reciprocal reaction. How do you feel about doing your part when your partner has already given 110 percent?

A classic example of this happened to a client of mine: a manufacturing company that produces appliances. The sales and production departments worked together to ensure stock was delivered on time to cover sales promotions. Things were going well, customers were buying appliances through the promotions, and back orders almost ceased to exist. Sales managers were making record bonuses, however, while the production managers were not seeing any change in their bonuses. When the partnership met, this gap was brought to the attention of the sales and production vice presidents. They were told that production managers and supervisors were starting to get angry that salespeople were making huge bonuses while they did all the hard work. The two partners decided to split the promotion sales bonuses evenly between production and sales to deal with the inequality and provide mutual benefits to both partners. As a result, the partnership between production and sales worked so well that after a two-year period, both groups got record high bonuses. The partnership moved from resolving a logistics issue to making design improvements based on customer feedback that sales passed along to manufacturing. The partnership worked so well, in fact, that the vice president of sales told me one day: "I can't even remember what it was like when we were not working together in partnership."

A SIMPLE FORMULA

You have the potential to be a great partner and to create successful, long-lasting, trustworthy, and mutually beneficial partnerships. The formula is simple. Again and again I have emphasized the importance of understanding yourself first. It all begins with you. You need to know what you want. You need to select a partner who can help you close the gap between what you can currently do and where you want to be. You need to follow a partnering process: the Partnership Continuum. You need to be sure to keep the task and relationship dynamics in balance. You need to practice the six attributes of high PQ. And you need to improve continuously by using the Plan–Do–Check–Act cycle.

Follow the outline I have used in this book. It works. Don't deviate and don't take shortcuts. Relationships take time to build; trust takes time to build; it takes time to communicate. But once you have laid the foundation, partnerships will create endless value for your business and build you smart alliances to successfully compete in the future.

Bardwick, J. *Danger in the Comfort Zone.* New York: AMACOM, 1991.

Bartlett, C., and Ghoshal, S. *Managing Across Borders.* Boston: Harvard Business School Press, 1998.

Beckhard, R., and Pritchard, W. *Changing the Essence: The Art of Creating and Leading Fundamental Change in Organizations.* San Francisco: Jossey-Bass, 1991.

Bolton, R. *People Skills.* New York: Simon & Schuster, 1979.

Bracey, H., Rosenblum, J., Sanford, A., and Trueblood, R. *Managing from the Heart.* New York: Delacorte Press, 1990.

Branden, N. *Self-Esteem at Work.* San Francisco: Jossey-Bass, 1998.

Burley-Allen, M. *Listening: The Forgotten Skill.* New York: Wiley, 1995.

Cappelli, P. *The New Deal at Work.* Boston: Harvard Business School Press, 1999.

Celente, G. *Trends 2000.* New York: Warner Books, 1997.

Charan, R., and Tichy, N. *Every Business Is a Growth Business.* New York: Times Books, 1998.

Cohen, W. *The Stuff of Heros.* Atlanta, Ga: Longstreet, 1998.

Cohen-Rosenthal, E., and Burton, C. *Mutual Gains: A Guide to Union-Management Cooperation.* New York: Praeger, 1987.

Conner, D. *Managing at the Speed of Change.* New York: Villard, 1992.

Covey, S. *Principle-Centered Leadership.* New York: Summit Books, 1991.

Crum, T. *The Magic of Conflict.* New York: Simon & Schuster, 1987.

Csikszenthimihalyi, M. *Flow: The Psychology of Optimal Experience.* New York: HarperPerennial, 1990.

Dana, D. *Talk It Out.* Amherst, Mass.: Human Resource Development Press, 1990.

Filley, A. *Interpersonal Conflict Resolution.* Glenview, Ill.: Scott, Foresman, 1975.

Francis, D., and Young, D. *Improving Work Groups.* San Diego, Calif.: San Diego University Associates Press, 1979.

Goldhaber, G. *Organizational Communication.* (4th ed.). Dubuque, Iowa: Wm. C. Brown, 1986.

Gordon, T. *Leader Effectiveness Training.* New York: Bantam Books, 1980.

Greider, W. *One World, Ready or Not.* New York: Simon & Schuster, 1998.

Heenan, D., and Bennis, W. *Co-Leaders: The Power of Great Partnerships.* New York: Wiley, 1999.

Hillman, J. *The Soul's Code: In Search of Character and Calling.* New York: Random House, 1996.

Horton, T., and Reid, P. *Beyond the Trust Gap: Forging a New Partnership Between Managers and Their Employees.* Homewood, Ill.: Business One Irwin, 1991.

Jandt, F. *Win-Win Negotiating: Turning Conflict into Agreement.* New York: Wiley, 1985.

Katzenbach, J. *The Work of Teams.* Boston: Harvard Business School Press, 1998.

Kelly, K. *New Rules for the New Economy.* New York: Viking Books, 1998.

Koch R. *The 80/20 Principle.* New York: Currency Doubleday, 1998.

Kohn, A. *No Contest: The Case Against Competition.* Boston: Houghton Mifflin, 1986.

Kotter, J. *Leading Change.* Boston: Harvard Business School Press, 1996.

Lau, J., and Jelinek, M. *Behavior in Organizations: An Experiential Approach.* Homewood, Ill.: Irwin, 1984.

Mackay, H. *Dig Your Well Before You're Thirsty.* New York: Doubleday, 1997.

Miller, S., Nunnally, E., and Wackman, D. *Talking Together.* Minneapolis, Minn.: Interpersonal Communications Programs, 1979.

Nadler, D. *Feedback and Organizational Development: Using Data-Based Methods.* Reading, Mass.: Addison-Wesley, 1977.

Orsburn, J., Moran, L., Musselwhite, E., and Zenger, J. *Self-Directed Work Teams: The New American Challenge.* Homewood, Ill.: Business One Irwin, 1990.

Renesch, J., and Defoore, B. (Eds.). *The New Bottom Line: Bringing Heart and Soul to Business.* San Francisco: NewLeaders Press, 1996.

Robbins, H. *Turf Wars: Moving from Competition to Collaboration.* Glenview, Ill.: Scott, Foresman, 1989.

Schaef, A., and Fassel, D. *The Addictive Organization.* San Francisco: Harper San Francisco, 1988.

Senge, P. *The Fifth Discipline.* New York: Doubleday Currency, 1990.

Shea, G. *Building Trust in the Workplace.* New York: AMA Management Briefing, 1984.

Sherman, A. *The Complete Guide to Running and Growing Your Business.* New York: Times Books, 1997.

Stanat, R. *Global Gold: Panning for Profits in Foreign Markets.* New York: AMACOM, 1998.

Stewart, D. *The Power of People Skills.* New York: Wiley, 1986.

Thomas, K. W., and Kilmann, R. H. *Thomas-Kilmann Conflict Mode Instrument.* Palo Alto, Calif.: XICOM, 1974.

Weisbord, M. *Productive Workplaces: Organizing and Managing for Dignity, Meaning, and Community.* San Francisco: Jossey-Bass, 1990.

Weisbord, M. *Discovering Common Grounds.* San Francisco: Berrett-Koehler, 1992.

Wheatley, M. *Leadership and the New Science: Learning About Organizations from an Orderly Universe.* San Francisco: Berrett-Koehler, 1992.

Woodward, H., and Buchholz, S. *Aftershock: Helping People Through Corporate Change.* New York: Wiley, 1987.

Increase your Partnering Intelligence with these easy-to-use, hands-on tools

Start with the assessment...

Partnering Quotient Assessment. Knowing your Partnering Quotient (PQ) is the first step to creating great partnerships. This assessment allows you to measure your own PQ, identify your strengths and weaknesses based on the six attributes of smart partners, and form an action plan for boosting your Partnering Intelligence. *10" x 8½", 20 pp.* (Item PI-001)

...then build the six attributes

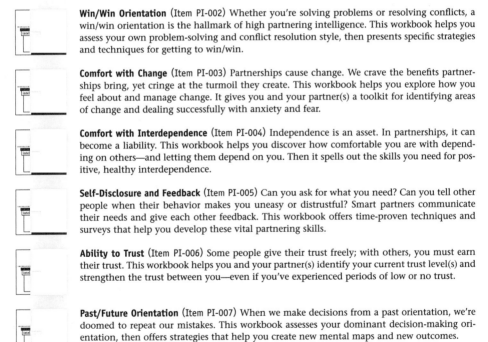

Win/Win Orientation (Item PI-002) Whether you're solving problems or resolving conflicts, a win/win orientation is the hallmark of high partnering intelligence. This workbook helps you assess your own problem-solving and conflict resolution style, then presents specific strategies and techniques for getting to win/win.

Comfort with Change (Item PI-003) Partnerships cause change. We crave the benefits partnerships bring, yet cringe at the turmoil they create. This workbook helps you explore how you feel about and manage change. It gives you and your partner(s) a toolkit for identifying areas of change and dealing successfully with anxiety and fear.

Comfort with Interdependence (Item PI-004) Independence is an asset. In partnerships, it can become a liability. This workbook helps you discover how comfortable you are with depending on others—and letting them depend on you. Then it spells out the skills you need for positive, healthy interdependence.

Self-Disclosure and Feedback (Item PI-005) Can you ask for what you need? Can you tell other people when their behavior makes you uneasy or distrustful? Smart partners communicate their needs and give each other feedback. This workbook offers time-proven techniques and surveys that help you develop these vital partnering skills.

Ability to Trust (Item PI-006) Some people give their trust freely; with others, you must earn their trust. This workbook helps you and your partner(s) identify your current trust level(s) and strengthen the trust between you—even if you've experienced periods of low or no trust.

Past/Future Orientation (Item PI-007) When we make decisions from a past orientation, we're doomed to repeat our mistakes. This workbook assesses your dominant decision-making orientation, then offers strategies that help you create new mental maps and new outcomes.

Contact The Partnership Continuum, Inc. directly for ordering and pricing information.
Quantity discounts are available.

The Partnership Continuum, Inc.
1201 Yale Place, Suite 1908 • Minneapolis, MN 55403-1960
Toll-free (U.S. and Canada): 888-292-0323 • Local: 612-375-0323 • Fax: 612-317-0713
Email: info@partneringintelligence.com • www.partneringintelligence.com